7 Principles of Divine Purpose!

Experiencing Power, Passion and True Success

By Randall Jay Brown

Published by Motivational Press, Inc.
7777 N Wickham Rd, # 12-247
Melbourne, FL 32940
www.MotivationalPress.com

Manufactured in the United States of America.

ISBN: 978-1-62865-072-3

CONTENTS

CHAPTER ONE
What if everything you believe about Success is wrong?!
Principle # 1: Resonance *15*

CHAPTER TWO
How to Access the "Flow" of True Success
Principle # 2: Universal Energy *55*

CHAPTER 3 ....
How to Reprogram your Conscious Mind to Raise your Frequency!
Principle #3: Choose Your Focus *95*

CHAPTER FOUR
How to Reprogram your Subconscious Mind for True Success!
Principle #4: Mind Renewal *148*

CHAPTER FIVE
How to Raise Your Frequency through Visualization!
Principle 5: Imagination *195*

CHAPTER SIX
How to Experience "The Flow" of Inspiration!
Principle #6: Inspiration *217*

CHAPTER SEVEN
How to Experience Mighty Change
Principle #7: Transformation *231*

FINAL WORDS *246*

RESOURCES AND REFERENCES *247*

The Purpose of this book: What's in it for you?

"Your work isn't to improve yourself, but to discover the magnificence that is already here, that you already are -- then to act from that vision."

–Derek Rydall

Dear reader, if you have picked up this book, perhaps you are much like the person who wrote to me saying,

"What advice would you give to someone who is absolutely overwhelmed and unhappy with their life circumstance in general. A person who has done all the wrong things for the right reasons and finds themself looking back and realizing that they have sold themselves out and short. How do you begin to change the circumstance that seems so insurmountable? And, how do you truly know what your 'divine purpose' is?"

If this is you, you are the person I am writing to.

If like most people, you're struggling with any of these challenges, my message will help!

- Limiting beliefs
- Self-doubts
- Feeling empty or without purpose
- Feeling disconnected spiritually
- Longing for something more
- Living without joy or passion
- Anxiety
- Avoiding life - hiding in addictions and self-defeating behaviors
- Depression and discouragement
- Stuck in a job you hate
- Making a living, but not living
- Feeling held-back or stuck

- Burned out
- Unemployed or under-employed
- Looking for an easier way
- This book is designed to help you:

Stop working at a job that smothers your spirit!

Stop struggling with the feelings that you were meant to be more!

Access the inner strength of your Divine Purpose!

Stop craving the approval of others!

Start making a living doing what you love!

Allow abundance into your life.

Improve your relationships.

What is Divine Purpose?

Divine Purpose is the divinely created masterpiece that lies inside of you. It is the unique greatness that has been planted in your DNA. It is a divine gift that flows effortlessly and freely, if you allow it to emerge. It is the "highest-good" that flows through you when you are connected to your source, God, Higher Power or whatever you understand it to be. It **is a joyful expression of your highest gift to humanity.**

Your Divine Purpose is the emergence of the dreams and passions that resonate so deeply inside you. It is a Divine energy that compels you to inspired-action, making you a visionary, inspired by a "calling" that is "meant to be." Your Divine Purpose is a gift so uniquely designed for you, that only you can do it in a way that it was intended.

Your Divine Purpose brings a deep sense of gratitude, fulfillment and well-being. It is your greatest opportunity for joy and happiness in this life!

What is True Success?

*"Just as Michelangelo believed God had already
done all the work, and his job was simply to see
the completed masterpiece imprisoned in that
block of stone and release it — take time today
to behold that masterpiece hidden in this block
of mortal stone... and set it free."*

– Derek Rydall

God has planted seeds of Divine Purpose in our souls! These seeds, if properly nourished, will bring forth an abundant harvest.

True success starts with the seed of a dream, desire or intention that begins to swell and enlarge your soul so that you can feel the swelling motions. The seed is good! Nourish it! As this divine seed takes root it has the potential to become a mighty tree.

True Success is different than the world's definition of success. True Success comes through aligning with your spiritual source, removing limiting beliefs and allowing your Divine Purpose to emerge. It is a success that flows effortlessly as a result of being who you were intended to be and not who society teaches you, you "should" be. It is focused on "How can I best utilize my God-given talents to serve humanity?"

The laws that govern this type of success are as immutable as the laws that govern the operation of nature, electricity or mathematics. True Success will always be the result when the laws by which it operates are followed.

True Success is:
- Being content with the masterpiece that God created you to be
- Being connected to your Divine Purpose and your True self
- Having a belief system free of limiting beliefs
- Experiencing the flow of inspiration
- Being transformed in a way that touches the lives of others

- Experiencing the deep meaning intended for your life
- Knowing your True self (your spiritual self)
- Knowing what brings you joy and passion
- Doing that which inspires you daily
- Living life "fully alive!"

True success is living in the flow of your Divine Purpose! Your Divine Purpose is a divinely created masterpiece that lies within you! True Success lies in understanding that everything you've been through and everything you are currently experiencing has purpose, and that purpose is to awaken you to your true identity and the unique greatness that lies within.

Although most of us have been taught success myths that disconnect us from True Success and Divine Purpose, the **Good News** is that by aligning with your Divine Purpose, or the person you were created to be, True Success will flow effortlessly! True Success can actually be yours by applying the 7 principles of Divine Purpose! The problem is not a lack of hard work, intelligence, formal education or will-power. The real problem is *resistance (or dissonance) to the* source of all abundance – God. We really only experience two states: resistance or surrender. Surrender is a state of connection to God, and resistance is fighting to do it alone. . As you read this book you will learn about ways that you might be resisting the flow of your life's purpose, the passion that you were endowed with and True Success you are intended to experience.

What has it cost you to remain disconnected? What has it done to your mental, emotional, and even physical health?

How has this inner discontent impacted your happiness, your connection to others, and your opportunities in the world? What will it cost you if things remain the same… a month from now… a year from now… five years from now?

Remember, the battle between our Divine Purpose trying to emerge and our resistance to it causes stress. The harder you try to succeed at things that are not aligned with your Divine Purpose, the more likely it is that you will miss out on the True Success that lies within!

Early in my sales career, my company gave each of the sales reps a personality test. When the results came back, they revealed that I was a Choleric personality type, which means I was the type of person who pushed myself, and others, to succeed. I remember feeling very proud of that. I believed that being "success-driven" was the very attribute that would make me highly successful. I couldn't have been more wrong! .

Through personal experience I have learned that "driven-ness" cannot lead to True Success. I spent 24 years of my life "striving" to be a top sales person, driven by a desperate need to be recognized with sales awards, bonus checks and incentive trips. I know now that my frantic efforts were an attempt to connect with something "outside" of myself that would make me feel whole and complete.

Driven-ness is based on the false assumption that you are inherently broken and in need of "fixing." Driven-ness is a desperate attempt to acquire something "outside yourself." If you are waiting for things to change from the outside, you will be waiting forever. Life happens through you, not to you.

Although this may be a new concept to you, it is true that inner *resistance* blocks the flow of abundant life. As you continue reading, you will see that your disconnection from the flow of True Success is the result of *dissonance* that affects your ability to resonate with your Divine Purpose.

If I were to tell you that your current results had little to do with how smart you are, how hard you work, or how well you've planned your life, you might find that goes against your current belief system. Remain open-minded to the fact that your current belief system is a big factor in your resistance to True Success.

The answer to unlocking your flow of True Success lies deep inside of you, and the solution requires learning how to release subconscious, emotional and spiritual resistance.

The pain I experienced by being stuck in my own "inner resistance" led me to seek answers. Because of that, this is what I know about you, the reader: I know you have a purpose. I know your purpose creates intense passion in you. I know that following your passion will lead to True Success. However, I also know that your inner resistance is creating a real barrier.

Here's my Guarantee:

If you will read this book and dedicate yourself to applying these principles, you will experience your Divine Purpose emerging in a way you cannot imagine.

You will learn to see through the myths that have kept you from True Success. You will learn how to connect with the Universal source of power from which True Success flows. You will learn how to reconnect with your true joy and passion. You will learn to choose beliefs, thoughts and emotions that empower you. You will learn how to reprogram your mind with empowering beliefs. You will learn how to create a clear vision of your purpose in life. You will learn how to take inspired actions that are aligned with True Success. You will be transformed into a new person.

What Makes this Book Unique?

"When you know yourself, you are empowered. When you accept yourself you are invincible." – Tina Lifford

Most personal development books and programs teach of your constant need to fix yourself. Self-improvement is a fallacy, a defense mechanism -- and it can never bring about lasting change. Even when we manage to improve this pseudo-self, we often feel more anxious and stressed, and under increased pressure to keep propping up this self-image that, deep down, we know is false.

By aligning with your Divine Purpose you will experience the flow of divine energy that unleashes the True Success that lies within.

True Success is found in aligning with your Divine Purpose. It comes by looking inside and discovering the unique set of gifts and talents that have been divinely encoded into your DNA.

Why I'm writing on this topic?

*"What lies behind us and what lies before us
are tiny matters compared to what lies within
us."*

— Ralph Waldo Emerson

I am writing this book because of my desire to share my journey. It has been a journey of discovering who I really am. I want you to know that no matter what you've been through, or what you are currently going through there is a masterpiece within you just waiting to emerge. This is absolutely true!

I've spent a good part of my life engaged in self-improvement hoping to "fix" myself. The more self-improvement work I did, the more broken and inadequate I began to feel. Finally I became aware that there is a part of me that doesn't need fixing; a part of me that has never been damaged. I finally discovered an alternative to trying to fix myself. I had to start allowing my true-self to emerge. On this journey, I've come to realize that we really don't solve our own problems; our problems actually dissolve as we evolve. None of us can really manipulate and manage our lives, but we can turn inside and discover what's really there!

Accessing the Divine Purpose within us is more like tuning our dial to the channel where the music is playing, and as we do, we come to realize that the music was playing all the time, we just weren't tuned in.

This book is intended to help you create the right circumstances to align energetically and mentally with the frequency of your Divine Purpose.

This is not a book centered on any specific religion, but I do recognize the existence of an actual being that I refer to as God, and I do use a few quotes from the Bible. . For the most part, this book is based on universal laws and spiritual principles. These laws and principles are always at work and they are in operation regardless of your beliefs or opinions. Universal laws are at work in both the visible (physical) and invisible (spiritual) realms.

In writing this book, I struggled to decide what to title it. I struggled particularly with whether to use the term Soul Purpose, Higher Purpose, Life Purpose or Divine Purpose.

I chose the term "Divine Purpose" because I believe universal principles are governed by a Source of divine power - God. Universal laws point to a Divine Source of energy and intelligence. This Divine Source is the creator of the divine system we refer to as the Universe.

This Divine Source is the fountain from which all good things flow. Access to this fountain or source is ours as we dissolve the barriers that resist its flow.

Some who have read this have said "this sounds like the 'Born Again' process referred to in religious teachings!" Yes, it is the spiritual journey that all world religions teach about. It is the transformational process that we are here to experience; it is our Divine Purpose!

Unfortunately, the vast majority of what we're taught directs us away from our true path. The obsessive drive to 'improve' ourselves not only takes us further from true fulfillment, and covers up our original perfection; it ingrains many of us with a sense that we're more broken than when we began. The very act of trying to improve ourselves often carries with it a seed of inadequacy that can **grow into a larger feeling of lack**, requiring greater attempts at self-improvement. It's like trying to dig yourself out of a hole – it just keeps getting deeper and deeper.

"We need only look to nature for clues about how we're really meant to grow. Does the acorn have to improve itself in order to become an oak? Does the caterpillar have to improve itself to become a butterfly? If the acorn could improve itself, it might become a better acorn, a stronger acorn – the best nut in the forest — but it would never become what it really is. Likewise, the caterpillar, through a self-improvement program, might become a faster, leaner, more beautiful caterpillar — but it would never fulfill its destiny to spread its wings and fly. The lack of awareness, or repression, of this authentic Self is at the root of the discontent most people

feel and the aggression that wreaks havoc on our planet." - Derek Rydall

"7 Principles of Divine Purpose" is not just a departure from what is found in self-help and success books. It is the complete opposite of what is often taught and what most people believe about how life works.

CHAPTER ONE

What if everything you believe about Success is wrong?!
Principle # 1: Resonance

"Everyone has a purpose in life . . . a unique gift or special talent to give to others. And when we blend this unique talent with service to others, we experience the ecstasy and exultation of our own spirit, which is the ultimate goal of goals."
– Deepak Chopra

Resonance – the Effortless Flow of Joy!

As a child, I knew exactly what brought me joy! It was playing baseball. The game was magical to me. I loved everything about it: the uniforms, the equipment, even the dimensions of the field. I loved the strategy of each pitch. I loved to watch the Major League players who had become my heroes for their amazing ability to play this magical game.

When I wasn't playing baseball, I was day-dreaming about baseball, reading books and articles about baseball. I would walk with my friends to 7-Eleven to buy baseball cards and baseball trading cups. I would buy baseball magazines so I could cut out the pictures and put them up on my bedroom wall.

I remember waking up on summer mornings so full of excitement! I could hardly wait to get outside and start a game.

Baseball *resonated* with me and there was a magical, joyful feeling that flowed through me when I played it. I knew I was born to play baseball.

No one ever had to motivate me to play baseball! My desire to play flowed as effortlessly as breathing. When I was playing baseball it was as if time didn't exist; I never checked the time to see when I needed to quit. It required no effort, no hard work and there was no pressure, no stress, just pure joy!

My Disconnection From Resonance

I grew up in a very normal, happy family, and to this day we are all very close and love each other deeply. My parents were loving and generous people who also happened to be extremely talented and high-achieving people. My Dad was gifted in athletics and business, while my mother was a gifted singer.

If there was a challenge in growing up with this "perfect" family it was, ironically, "perfectionism." Somewhere during those early years,

I accepted the belief that I had to live up to my parents' abilities and accomplishments. I believed that I HAD to excel, in the same way, and at the same things they did, in order to be worthy of love and acceptance.

Somewhere along the way I lost the ability to feel "fully alive." As anxiety and fear of failure crept into my life, I began avoiding many of the joys of life, in order to avoid the potential pain of disappointment.

Along the way I came to the conclusion that there were only two standards of performance: perfection or failure, there was no middle ground. This caused me to drive myself very hard and to put a lot of internal pressure on myself. In doing so, I became my own harsh judge.

By the time I reached high school, the inner pressure of perfectionism had me completely disconnected from my earlier, pure love of baseball. The passion that had once resonated so strongly, had been whittled away, one perfectionistic piece at a time. I became terrified of not living up to my own perfectionistic ideals, no longer playing for the joy of the game, but instead trying to avoid failing, because failure, of any kind, was not an option. What could I do but try even harder, which brought on more stress and anxiety.

My first year of high school I was chosen for one of the developmental teams, but in the first game I made two errors and struck out three times because of the mental tension I was under. In my mind, this was completely unacceptable, and I sunk into a feeling of despair I had never before experienced.

When I tried out the next year, I was so anxious to succeed, and so fearful of making a mistake, that I could hardly function. Baseball was no longer an "effortless flow."

In college, I did what I felt I "should" do by pursuing a major in Business, which I had no passion for. In fact, it caused me great anxiety, and when I didn't excel in my school work, I experienced frustration and discouragement.

When I graduated, I followed in my Dad's footsteps and went into sales. By now I was completely disconnected from what brought me joy, and was completely without a dream or passion in my life. I was just following the steps I believed "I should" follow.

Of course, I took on my sales career with the same perfectionistic mindset. My focus was completely "outside-in!" I needed the recognition, the bonus checks and the awards that are typical of people needing to be motivated to do something that doesn't inspire them.

Under the stress of needing to be a high-performer, I began having panic attacks and severe depression. Somehow I continued in sales for many years, all the time driving myself, and continuously battling anxiety. Eventually OCD and addictive tendencies began to take over, and I hit the wall. I knew there had to be something more. I had reached the point of emotional and spiritual bankruptcy.

Even the financial benefits of being in sales began to diminish. Eventually I found myself headed toward financial bankruptcy.

My Reconnection to Resonance

The direction of my life began to change when I had an amazing spiritual experience. One Sunday afternoon as I was praying in my bedroom, being now truly desperate, something seemed to subtly shift and a gentle message pierced my despair. I received the impression that we needed to move to Utah where my father-in-law worked as a personal success coach for the Professional Education Institute, a company that helps clients all over the world align with their dreams and passions.

Things didn't completely change overnight, there were still challenges ahead, but my transformation process was underway. Little by little, I was exposed to the success principles taught by some of the world's top personal development gurus.

After working there for a while, it became evident that there was something absolutely vital missing from their materials. True Success flows as we align with who we are created to be – our Divine Purpose!

While working at PEI, I had the opportunity of meeting best-selling author and inspirational speaker Jack Canfield. In his presentation, he took us through a meditation exercise designed to help us connect with our "Highest Good." This simple exercise had a life-changing effect on me. For years I had an inner desire to become an author myself. I had started and stopped several times in my efforts to write a book. As Jack spoke to us that day, something amazing took place inside of me that caused powerful emotions to *resonate*. I know now that these feelings that resonated so powerfully inside of me were the whisperings of my "Divine Purpose."

This experience caused me to ask myself, **"What if everything I've believed about success is wrong?"**

What if True Success is a measure of how happy I am? What if True Success is less about effort and more about allowing? What if True Success flows as the result of a Divine Purpose designed for my life?

As you apply the principle of *resonance* you will realize that True Success is not based on man-made success principles. You will understand that True Success is based on principles that are universal and eternal, and you will come to know that True Success is based on "Principles of Divine Purpose!"

This is why so many "success-driven" people are actually programmed to fail and why so many people who purchase personal development courses, books, and audio programs don't experience any real transformation.

> *"When Life calls us, that's when we have to answer,"* . . . *When people ask me how I've accomplished everything I've done, I just say I've answered the telephone and opened the mail and did what was in front of me. That's*

how I lived. It was as if Life simply took care of everything one step at a time." - Louise Hay

"Today so many people want fast success. But when we're on the spiritual path and responding to what Life presents us, I think the most powerful work we do happens gradually over time."

— Louise Hay

True Success is The Flow of Divine Purpose

"Success is so much more than money. Real success is a feeling of being fulfilled, knowing that your life has purpose and meaning. It's trading your life for what you love and what you believe in; giving your very best in that pursuit. Show me someone who is doing this, and I'll show you a successful person!"

— John Assaraf

The Meaning of Flow

Have you experienced moments when everything just seems to flow? Moments when you didn't have to struggle or fight or force things to happen? Flow is the mental state in which a person is fully immersed in a feeling of energized focus, full involvement, and enjoyment. You've probably witnessed times when an athlete, like Michael Jordan, is "in the flow." When people enter this state they are able to effortlessly do amazing things.

Flow is a state of total absorption in a given activity to the point of being in a near meditative state. It can be great for your mental health and wellness. Finding "flow" in your work, play and daily life can create considerably greater life satisfaction as well.

Flow is Effortless

Everything in creation has come from one universal source of energy, and that is the source from which True Success flows. When you're in a state of effortless "flow," you are experiencing True Success!

Flow occurs when you are focused on purpose. If your desire for success is focused on, "How can I best utilize my God-given talents to serve humanity?", then your success is based on your Divine Purpose. Divine Purpose produces one-ness, connection and resonance with God, (Divine Source) and with others. This type of success has an "inside-out" focus. An "inside-out" focus is looking to the inner greatness planted in our spiritual DNA. It is looking to the spiritual self that lies within, and its capacity to receive inspiration and intuition from a higher source.

An "outside-in" focus comes from the belief that you are needing something outside of your self in order to be whole. It comes from the assumption that you need fixing and something outside of your true-self can do that for you. It is looking for answers outside of the spiritual-self inside you that has divine greatness planted deep inside.

Effort-ful success occurs when you are ego-focused. If your desire for success is focused on, "What's in it for me?", your success will be effort-ful because your concept of success is ego-based. Ego produces separation, disconnection and dissonance from God, or Divine Source. This type of success has an "outside–in" focus.

Ask yourself this question: "If I had all the money and all the time I could ever want, what would I do?" Would you choose to do what you are currently doing? If not, it is because you are not aligned with your *Divine Purpose*. You are not aligned with your passion, and that keeps you from expressing your God-given talents in ways that bring you joy.

The experience I had with Jack Canfield was my Divine Purpose resonating, calling me to live my passion.

Each of us has a gift, or talent that flows effortlessly. That gift or talent is part of your Divine Purpose. When you use your Divine

Purpose to meet the needs of others, abundance flows. Your life becomes a manifestation of True Success!

Aligning with Divine Purpose brings the flow of true greatness. The enabling power to become a great parent, a great spouse, a great leader, a great employee, a great friend, a great business person flows freely.

Your Divine Purpose is going to make you great; it's going to release an effortless flow of power into your life, and it's going to open doors you didn't know existed.

How do I Reconnect to Resonance

"The meaning of life is to find your gift. The Purpose of life is to give it away."
— *Pablo Picasso*

Too many people are under the false impression that external things will purchase them joy, and that cannot be further from the truth. To illustrate this, let me ask you three questions.

1. What do you want right now more than anything else?
2. If you were to get number one, what would that do for you? What would that change in your life?
3. If you were to get your wish how would you feel?

What you really want more than anything else is not how you answered number one. It's how you answered number three. I find that most people answer question number one with an external circumstance – money, health, fame, career, house, new car, whatever, while very few people answer the question with an internal state like love, joy, or peace. This is because most people don't believe they can have the internal state without first achieving the external circumstance. In other words, most people believe that if they achieve fame, wealth etc., the love, joy, peace, or freedom that they really want will naturally follow. Actually, the opposite is the truth. If you seek for a higher internal state (love, joy, peace etc.) you will begin to resonate with your dreams and passions, inspiration will begin to flow and the outward things (money, career, possessions etc.) will be a natural result.

This is why so many success programs are in violation of True Success. External expectations are killers of our happiness, because the instant you have an external circumstance as your goal, it puts you into an immediate chronic state of stress until you either get that thing or don't get it. And stress is a significant   contributor to illness and disease.

So what is the number one goal in your life? If it is an external circumstance it will cause you to fail! Even if you made a million dollars you would be unhappy because of the stress, and the internal will-power needed can never be sustained. This is not True Success! You are violating your Divine Purpose. Your Divine Purpose comes from inside.

Step one: Do what brings you joy

> *"People suffer when they pursue a life or chase a*
> *dream that doesn't belong to them"*
> *- Carolyn May*

Life is too short to continue living a joyless life! How do you want to spend your days? A high percentage of people are spending their days doing things they don't like doing. They are tip-toeing through life hoping to get safely to death. This is your life! If you are spending your days doing something you don't like to do – WAKE UP AND LIVE! ACT AS IF IT'S IMPOSSIBLE TO FAIL!

Look deep inside and ask yourself "What brings me joy?" Whatever that is, that is what you are meant to experience. You were created to follow your joy. Make the commitment to discover what brings you joy and do it every day, even if it's just for a few minutes.

The things that bring you joy are given to you to guide you to your Divine Purpose. Begin opening your life to more and more of these things.

If you are just making a living, instead of living, I challenge you to start looking at how you can take your joy and turn it into a business of your own.

When I talk about living your joy, people immediately respond by saying "What if I have to work at a job? I have to pay my bills!" There are no "have to's." Everything is a choice. It's the belief that you don't have a choice that is the problem.

Without knowing the principle of resonance, you cannot understand the idea of your career becoming your calling, and you will continue looking outside yourself for a "job."

By fully aligning with spiritual principles your career will emerge from a purpose and passion that isn't separate from who you are, but is rather an extension of who you are.

It's not my purpose in this book to teach you how to start your own business, but if you're ready to begin living your passion, I definitely recommend that you get a copy of the book "Why Now is the Time to Crush it! Cash In On your Passion" by Gary Vaynerchuk; as well as the book "Platform – Get Noticed in a Noisy World" by Michael Hyatt.

There is an open window of opportunity right now that we have never seen in history. There is no reason, in the day and age we live in, that people can't take their passion and with the power of the internet and social media connect with an audience of people that share that passion, and provide them information, services or products that they are really looking for.

There is no reason to stay stuck! Take your passion and open your mind to the information that will allow you to serve your flock of followers and in time you will have a business that you are so passionate about that you can't wait to get out of bed to get going. When you feel that way, you can't help but succeed. If taking this step is out of your comfort zone, hold on. We'll get to comfort zones and limiting beliefs in an upcoming chapter.

If the idea of creating a business doesn't appeal to you, at least begin the practice of taking time to do something you love every day, and soon you'll experience a flow of inspiration that will guide you.

Step two: Avoid success-myths

> *"Men occasionally stumble over the truth, but*
> *most of them pick themselves up and hurry off*
> *as if nothing happened."*
>
> - Winston Churchill

If you are disconnected from the flow of joy, it's probably because of the success myths you have accepted. Many of the things that society teaches us about success are actually things that disconnect us from *resonance*.

I start out this chapter by asking an important question, *"What if everything you believe about success is wrong?!"* I ask that question because of the "spiritual dyslexia" we have developed in our culture. We live in a world where people are rewarded for working long hours at the expense of a balanced and healthy life.I In doing so, they are approaching success with an "outside-in" focus rather than looking for the answers that come from within.

The thing that makes this book unique and different from other personal development books is that it approaches success from the "inside-out." Any philosophy that teaches success from the "outside-in" is in opposition to Universal laws. True success, the effortless flow of Divine Purpose, always works from the "inside out."

The energy we broadcast out into the universe draws to itself energies that are of an equal frequency, resonance, or vibration. In other words, where your attention goes, your energy flows.

I think another way of defining this Universal law would be to say that: resonant energies or frequencies are divinely designed to work in harmony.

Vibrational signals have the capacity to harmonize with some frequencies while clashing with others. The Universe we are a part of was divinely created to work that way.

Resonance occurs when one vibrational signal **accepts or aligns** with other frequencies. Dissonance results when frequencies **clash, or *resist*** each other. This definition means that there are certain vibrational signals that work well together and others that don't. These frequencies don't have to be exactly the same in order to resonate.

Musical notes are said to be in resonance when they harmonize. They may be different pitches in different ranges, yet they create a beautiful sound when they are put together. For instance, notes from the Bass staff may resonate with notes from the Treble staff.

Many people who try to apply "the Law of Attraction" believe that focusing on something they want with strong emotion will cause it to manifest. Unfortunately, people apply that with an "outside-in" focus. They are focused on the external things that they perceive are missing from their lives rather than focusing on allowing their true greatness to emerge. But I submit this question: What if the vibrational energy of the thing you want to "attract" is dissonant from the vibrational signal of your true spiritual self? What if it is not aligned with the Divine Purpose that your creator encoded into your DNA? The answer is easy! There will be dissonance! And dissonance never produces purpose, passion and True Success.

Resonance is experienced as we apply our passions and gifts to the

Divine Purpose for which we are created! The Universe will support us in our unique gifts and talents, and direct us through divine inspiration.

Your spirit and your subconscious mind know your Divine Purpose and they know what is best for you. As you begin to align with your Divine Purpose, there may be a transition period, where it seems like things are falling apart. This just means that the things that are not aligned with your Divine Purpose are beginning to fall away.

When it feels like things are falling apart, things are really falling into place. This is why so many people say "I tried the Law of Attraction and it didn't work for me."

Divine Purpose cannot flow when there is dissonance, and True Success only happens when there is resonance.

We are always resonating with something, good or bad, and we are always manifesting results of some kind, but when we look inside and listen to who we are called to be, we resonate with the things that bring Purpose, Passion and True Success.

Our "spiritually dyslexic" society perpetuates a lot of myths that keep us pursuing uninspired paths that keep us focusing on success with an "outside-in" focus. These success-myths lead us away from the resonance of True Success and Divine Purpose. Here are just a few:

Myth #1 – Success is Determined by Human Potential

"When you are inspired by a Great Purpose,
everything will begin to work for you."
- Wayne Dyer

No matter how talented and gifted a person may be, human potential on its own is limited. It is only when the ego that separates us from our Divine Source (God), is laid aside, that our true potential becomes limitless. True potential and True Success cannot be realized until ego is laid aside, allowing us to resonate with a higher power. The submission of our own will means giving away the only thing that is truly ours to give.

Each of us has a story, and the common thread in each of our stories is that the opposition inherent in mortality will at times expose us to our "extremities." Whether it be the death of a loved one, the loss of financial security, the loss of physical health, or addiction, life is designed to bring us to the "end of ourselves," to help us turn to the a power far beyond our own, a power that is the Source of the True Success designed for us. As we connect with that Higher Power we will find that our life has a purpose that flows from that divine connection.

True Success, your Divine Purpose, is experienced only as we align with a Divine Source, God, a Higher Power or whatever you understand it to be. **What makes True Success unique is that it is based on our need for divine help.**

True Success is not just philosophy; it is based on universal laws. The Biblical teaching: "*As a man thinketh in his heart so is he,*"(Proverbs 23:7) correlates with the universal law that states: "*thought is vibration.*" Christ's teaching that, "*All things are possible to him that believeth*"(Mark 9:23) is congruent with the idea that, "*Our focus can harness the energy that creates worlds.*" Both are focused on a transformation that takes place from the "inside-out."

In 1957, Earl Nightingale recorded his famous classic - "The Strangest Secret," in which he taught the Universal truth that: "*You become what you think about.*" Napoleon Hill taught the concept of, "*Think and Grow Rich.*" Now thirty-five years later, Paulo Coelho described the same idea in his novel The Alchemist: "*When you want something, all the universe conspires in helping you achieve it.*"

The Alchemist in the novel is a mystical chemist who can perform the feat of taking lead and making it into gold. Like Alchemy, universal laws work from the "inside out," with the potential to transform us into gold.

Your Divine Purpose has a powerful signal that is designed for you, and as you *tune-in* to it, success will flow effortlessly. That is how resonance works!

It is somewhat similar to how radio waves work. Even though we are unaware of them, radio signals are all around us. It's only when a radio is *tuned-in* to those signals that we become consciously aware of them. That is how resonance works!

If we take two tuning forks of the same pitch, or frequency, and place them near each other, by striking one of them, we send sound waves traveling through the air that cause the other fork to vibrate as well. The tuning forks are now resonating with each other. However, if we use tuning forks of different frequencies, resonance does not occur. If the frequency of one matches the frequency of the other, it picks up its vibrations. That is resonance! Resonance occurs when energy frequencies align.

True success resonates at the spiritual level. It works from the "inside out." Resonance is a universal principle that works the same at the spiritual level, as it does at the physical, only at much higher frequencies.

Resonance with the flow of Divine Purpose requires an "inside out" focus similar to what Jack Canfield helped me experience with his meditation exercise.

I once saw a science experiment where a scientist passed a million volts of electricity through his body without experiencing physical harm. Normally a million volts of electricity would kill a person instantly, but he was able to do it by changing the electrical energy frequency so that it was dissonant from the energy of his body. By doing so the electricity passed through his body without resonating. When vibrational frequencies are dissonant they simply pass each other by.

This is why some people can't seem to connect with True Success. The energy of their thoughts and emotions are dissonant from the flow of Higher Power. The signal of their Divine Purpose passes them by, without their awareness, because of their dissonance.

Myth #2 – Success Is the Result of What We "Do"

Early in my sales career I was driven by an "outside-in" focus. My need for the external rewards of success (sales awards, bonuses, incentive trips) was so high that I was willing to set aside purpose and meaning in order to be rewarded and recognized. My "outside-in" focus had me buying into a success-myth.

Success-myths are   ideas and philosophies that create dissonance to the flow of a Higher Power. A success-myth that affected me for many years, is found in a popular booklet titled, "The Common Denominator of Success," which contains this famous quote: *the secret of success lies in the fact that successful people form the habit of **doing** things failures don't like to **do**.*" (Albert E.N. Gray, Common Denominator of Success). The interesting thing about success-myths is that they often contain half-truths. They contain elements of truth, while leaving out the Universal Principles.

The quote leads you to assume that if you'll just **do** the things that unsuccessful people aren't willing to **do**, you will be successful. Focusing primarily on "**doing**" is an "outside-in" focus.

Rather than focusing on "what unsuccessful people aren't willing to do," what if we focused on: "If time and money weren't an issue what would I become? Would I continue to do what I'm doing now?" If not, you are not experiencing *resonance.*

Too many people are focused on **doing,** and they are miserable. Misery is not True Success, it is dissonance! True success flows from the things that bring us joy.

Why doesn't the "**do**" always lead to the desired "*have?*" It's because the "**do,**" on its own, will not do much, unless it's preceded by "**be.**"

An "inside-out" focus centers on *"being"* and Divine Purpose is about *"being"* who we were intended to *"be."*

This myth is perpetuated by ego, which Dr. Wayne Dyer says, is the idea that "who I am is separate from God, my source."[1] When we believe we are separate, we start to believe "I am what I **do**, I am what I have, I am separate from everybody else, I am my reputation, I am what is missing in my life." There are too many people doing what they "should" instead of being who they are.

In making this point I am in no way saying there will not be "doing" involved in True Success. True success is not the result of just taking massive action; it is the result of taking inspired-action based on a Divine Purpose that is aligned with your authentic self! An obsessive focus on "doing" causes resistance to the flow of True Success.

"You have a unique talent and a unique way of expressing it. There is something that you can do better than anyone else in the world – and for every unique talent and unique expression of that talent, there are also unique needs. When these needs are matched with the creative expression of your talent that is the spark that creates affluence. Expressing your talents to fulfill needs creates unlimited wealth and abundance." [2]

True success is about being who we truly "are," and who we "are determines what actions we will be inspired to take. As you will see in later chapters, being true to who we are and allowing the flow of inspiration must come before "doing."

You don't need to chase success! Just **be** the best version of yourself and success will chase you!

Myth # 3 – Success is Achieved Through Will-Power.

> *"Divine Purpose is not something you achieve it*
> *is something you connect to."*

Most people try to change their lives through will-power. The problem with that is that "will-power" doesn't really work. It is only our conscious attention trying to override our subconscious programming. For example if someone makes the decision that they are going to quit smoking, they probably will not smoke – for a while, but as soon as they run into stress the subconscious mind says, "you smoke" and the next thing they know they have a cigarette in their hand.

The same is true if you're on a diet. When you use what you call "will-power," eventually your will-power breaks, then your subconscious mind takes over and you find yourself with cheesecake in your hand. The subconscious will keep you following the blueprint that it has been programmed with.

This is why a great majority of people who invest in wealth building courses remain broke. As soon as their conscious mind gets distracted by people, situations and problems, they stop applying the wealth creation principles and the subconscious blueprint takes over again. It's not because they have no will-power, it's because they're using the wrong part of their minds to make the change!

This is what causes people to become stuck, in spite of the fact that their conscious attention is focused on success.

The reason goal setting often falls short is that most people set goals by purely focusing on will-power. It is "outside-in" focused and "ego-driven." It's based on myths about what you believe you "should do" and ignores the calling of your true-self - your spirit. "Ego-driven" goal setting is always a temporary solution, because you must continually motivate yourself in order to sustain it.

On the other hand, goal setting from an "inside-out" approach is based on the flow of inspiration, passion and joy that come from within. This approach includes your spiritual calling and is driven by Divine Purpose. It requires no motivation to sustain, because it flows through divine inspiration.

When you set a goal, you do it with your conscious mind. Your conscious mind is the "goal setter," but it is your subconscious mind that is the "goal getter." Without releasing the dissonance and limiting beliefs in your subconscious mind, it will override the goal you are holding in your conscious mind. We will talk more about how to overcome mental dissonance in a later chapter.

Success is too often defined as the achievement of a desired goal that is measured in terms of money, fame, position, accolades, or achievements. There are many aspects to success; material wealth is just one of them. True Success is not something we arrive at, it is a journey! Monetary abundance can make the journey more enjoyable, but True Success includes health, passion, relationships, mental health, emotional peace and spiritual well-being.

. Your Divine Purpose promises strength in areas where you are lacking. It leads you on paths you would not expect to take, and brings people into your life you would not expect to meet. "Your Divine Purpose is God's plan for your life. In the end, the value of your life will not be determined by your accomplishments, but by what God has been able to accomplish through you."[3] True success is something you "**allow**" into your life by "tuning in" to a source of guidance that goes by many names—God, spirit, higher power, inner guide, intuition, inspiration and Divine Purpose. **When Divine Purpose is flowing into your life you are truly successful!**

True success, is what we are here to experience! It is the reason for our existence.

In the "Common Denominator of Success," Albert Gray did go on to mention that we need a purpose in order to develop the habits of doing what the unsuccessful won't do. But a purpose that does not flow from a Higher Source is insufficient! True Success flows when your Divine Purpose Is resonating with your spiritual Source - God. (We'll learn more about Source energy in chapter two.)

Divine Purpose is less about "frantic maneuvering" and more about **allowing.** Here are some examples of thoughts that create dissonance:

- "I have to make this happen or it won't happen"
- "I'm not working hard enough at this"
- "I'll make this happen myself"

These types of thoughts work against True Success, because they don't **allow** the principle of resonance to work. These types of thoughts produce emotions of "struggle" and "lack" that send out a signal that is dissonant to abundance.

Allowing means:
- Letting go
- Letting God, or a higher power work in your life.
- Waiting on inspiration and divine timing.
- Believing
- Remaining detached from immediate results.
- Releasing negative beliefs, thoughts and emotions.
- Receiving

The sooner you are ready to connect and allow, the sooner you will experience True Success flowing into your life.

Myth #4 – Success Requires Knowing "How-To"

"It's God's job to provide 'the way,' it's our job to choose our focus."

There is a big difference between "planning your life" and having a "design for your life." A designed life is centered on your dreams and passions; it is Divine Purpose-driven, and is aligned with your spiritual calling. We have been trained to think that "if we don't have a plan, we plan to fail," but when we align our trueself, we don't need to know all the "how-to's." The plan will come through inspiration. When you have a vision that is filled with emotion, the Universe begins to deliver a plan to you. If you've been spinning your wheels for years trying to intellectualize a plan and nothing is working for you, that should tell you something.

The Wright Brothers had a dream of being able to fly. Even though they had no idea how to do it, they knew it was their "ultimate calling" to bring it to pass.

Likewise we don't need to know every step of our journey in advance. We can tap into an intelligence that is much greater than our own. I know this is a huge leap for people who are analytical and skeptical. I know it was for me.But when I realized that my way of doing things wasn't working, I decided it was time to follow my intuition. Let go of the "how to" and pay attention to what the Universe is delivering to you.

Instead of focusing on not knowing every step, get really clear on what you really want. If you have the mindset of, "I'm going to solve this problem," that is where you will stay emotionally and energetically, and that is what you're going to resonate with.

Start taking action on the ideas, people and opportunities that begin to manifest in your life, and as you do, it will create a chain of events. You will start meeting people, finding information and opportunities that suddenly appear. Once you're in this "flow," things start to happen very quickly. And when you're in the "flow," things always seem to work out for you.

This is more of a "way of being," than it is a process. It's about getting clear everyday on what you want your life to "be."

"Being" means honoring the things that bring bliss and joy into your life. It all comes back to having a vision that inspires you. It is so important to take time every day to do things that inspire you. Even though it may seem like this is a waste of time and not solving any of your problems - it is!

When you take time to enjoy the things you love every day, it has a very powerful effect, and the more you stay there the more your environment will change. Enjoy the things that make you feel good, and be OK with that.   Do not allow yourself to feel guilty about it. It's important to feel good. The more you follow your passion and work toward something that inspires you, the more things will start to change. You will just have to trust this. It's one of those things that you may not believe until you try it.

There are techniques we will talk about later in this book that will help you release resistance and re-program limiting beliefs, but a lot of those things happen naturally and fall away once you align with who you are meant to "be."

The most important thing is to get clear on what you really love and what you are really passionate about. Spend more time each day enjoying those things and watch what happens.

When inspiration comes inspired action will naturally follow. Trust that the Universe is giving you something that aligns with your passion.

Most personal development programs create a process of trying to map out every step, and that process leaves out divine assistance.

Planning out every step of your life without the flow of inspiration does not produce True Success. This is an "outside-in" focus which in and of itself is nothing more than "ego."

Life planning without divine assistance is much like expecting a tiny seed to grow into a fruit bearing tree, without sunlight. Although the seed's purpose is to grow into a tree that will eventually bring forth fruit, it is impossible without sunlight. Universal laws are the God-given system that makes growth and transformation possible.

"Seeds of greatness" have been sown into each one of us, but without the flow of a Higher Power transformation cannot occur.

Success-myths omit the need for a power beyond our own, because they are not based on universal principles!

Myth #5 – Hard Work Equals Success

"Success is the ability to fulfill your desires with effortless ease."

– Deepak Chopra

New studies show that people are willing to work harder for their own self-directed purpose than they are for any type of financial incentive. This shows that the joy of doing something deeply meaningful and purposeful is far more inspiring than having a carrot dangled in front of us by an employer. The key is that when we are aligned with our purpose, it doesn't seem like work because we are in a state of flow.

When we live and breathe our Divine Purpose, there is no longer a need to differentiate between our work life and our personal life, because we're living in the effortless flow of our passion.

A lot of talented people who have been born with great gifts and talents have eventually found themselves "stuck." They are frustrated, miserable and not succeeding. Why? Because they aren't being true to who they are meant to be; they aren't being what they were born to be.

There are too many people who haven't learned that they don't have to settle! No one in the day and age we live in needs to settle for working at a job they hate, or for working at something they have no passion for, just to pay the bills.

Have you ever wondered why some people seem to get incredible results with seemingly little effort, while others achieve so little while putting forth so much effort? Some of the most intelligent and talented people I know have a hard time putting food on the table. It's almost as if some invisible barrier is holding them back.

Why do some people seem to have the magic touch? You've heard people say. "Everything he touches turns to gold." And have you ever noticed that a person who becomes successful tends to continue to become more successful – and, on the other hand, have you noticed how someone who's a struggling tends to continue to struggle?

"We need a more spiritual approach to success and to affluence, which is the abundant flow of all good things to you." [4]

"If you observe nature at work, you will see that least effort is expended. Grass doesn't try to grow, it just grows. Fish don't try to swim, they just swim. Flowers don't try to bloom, they bloom. Birds don't try to fly, they just fly. This is their intrinsic nature. The earth doesn't try to spin on its axis; it is the nature of the earth to spin with dizzying speed and hurtle through space. It is the nature of babies to be in bliss. It is the nature of the sun to shine. It is the nature of stars to glitter and sparkle. And it is human nature to make our dreams manifest into physical form, easily and effortlessly."[5] Your Divine Purpose, is not something you try to do, it is who you are! That is why it flows effortlessly! That is why it is "True Success!"

Unless you follow the things that bring you joy you are resisting Universal laws. That resistance is what causes life to feel like a struggle. By learning to embrace the power of universal laws, you can create anything you desire. "You can still get results through effort and through trying, but at a cost. The cost is stress, heart attacks and the compromised function of your immune system." [6] The things that we call miracles are actually Universal Laws in effect. On the other hand, striving for success that is not aligned with your Divine Purpose is effortful. When you live in harmony with the Universal Laws, action becomes effortless. It's not that you aren't taking action. Your actions are smarter, they are more inspired and more joyful because they "flow" from a Divine Source.

For people like me who have spent their lives trying too hard, this is a difficult concept to believe. True Success – your Divine Purpose, starts on the inside and moves outward. It involves doing what you love to do and doing it in a way that brings you the most joy.

When you align with a Higher Purpose, True Success simply flows with less effort. This is because your actions are inspired by joy. Joyful action multiplies your energy, enabling you to create anything you want, including unlimited wealth.

Trying harder and working longer is not the key to financial transformation. Instead this leads to physical and emotional burnout. To break through to True Success, you must retrain your brain to get rid of your negative limiting beliefs, habits and behaviors — and you must reinforce the right positive ones to allow "flow" to occur.

As you follow your passion a channel of inspiration is opened, inspiring you to take actions that seem effortless. True success is a connection to everything you need to leave your legacy in the world.

Resonance is the effortless flow of everything you need!

Myth #6 – Formal Education is Essential to Success

"Formal education will make you a living; self-education will make you a fortune."

\- Jim Rohn

I know of a man, who from the time his children were young, taught them that he never, ever wanted them to worry about making a living. He told them that if they were unable to make a living when they grew up, he would provide for them, they were not to worry about it. He also told them that he didn't want them to focus on doing well in school or worrying about getting the best grades or going to the best colleges. He told them that what he really wanted them to focus on was asking themselves how they can best serve humanity and what their unique talents were.

He taught his children that they each had a unique talent and their own special way of expressing that talent. Interestingly, his kids ended up going to the best schools, getting the best grades, and even in college they were financially self-sufficient, because they were focused on their purpose and their path unfolded naturally. This is True Success! This is Divine Purpose!

Most of us were probably taught that success comes from working hard in school, getting good grades and getting a job with a good company. However, many highlysuccessful people have recognized that a life of job dependency could never align with their purpose and passions.

Don't get me wrong, I am not against formal education. My college days are some of the fondest memories of my life. But an Ivy League degree isn't needed for true success. "Top academic institutions are wonderful, but there are unrecognized benefits to not coming out of one. Grads from top schools are funneled into high-income 80-hour-per-week jobs, and 15-30 years of soul-crushing work is accepted as the default path."[7] For many people this path ends up in a dissonant life of being grossly over-worked and hating every minute of it.

The word "education" comes from the Latin word "educo" which means to develop or grow from within. This is a sacred process. It is not getting information; it is becoming aware of what is already within you. The way for you to have everything you want already exists, you just have to connect to it.

The incredible technology we have today has always existed; the "flow" of it just had to be aligned with.

Formal education is great, but "true success" comes from gaining the "flow" of specific knowledge intended for your Life's Purpose! This is the knowledge that leads to True Success! This is the knowledge that allows us to best serve humanity with our unique gifts and talents; it is the knowledge of how to tap into the energy that "flows" from a Divine Source.

Bob Proctor

Many of you may know Bob Proctor from the movie "the Secret." He is one of the top personal development gurus in the world. His formal education includes a grand total of two months of high school education. But because he learned the concept of changing his vibrational frequency to match his purpose and passion, he soon began seeing financial abundance flowing into his life.

Bob has no degrees, but he knows how to make a lot of money. Bob teaches large audiences around the world that hard work is the worst way to make a lot of money. The hard work paradigm is why only 3% of the population is making all the money. He teaches that if you learn to "think right" you can create your own economy. This type of thinking is not taught in schools.

Most people assume that we must move systematically from our current level of achievement to the next - one level at a time. For most of us, advancing at a measured pace – step by step - feels easier, but our lives simply don't have to operate that way. In certain areas of our lives we can think in terms of skipping levels. That is in sync with the higher side of your being. That is in perfect sync with the spiritual essence of who you are. ALL THINGS ARE POSSIBLE!

Quantum leaps in your performance can come without apparent effort and without time-controlling struggle, but you have to get to the other side of your logic. Quantum leaps require a radical departure from some of your current habits. A habit is merely an idea that is fixed in your subconscious mind.

Steve Jobs

"Have the courage to follow your heart and intuition. They somehow already know what you truly want to become."

– Steve Jobs

Most of us recognize the name Steve Jobs. Steve became the greatest creator of technology and the most influential executive of our time.

At a very young age, Steve showed an innate interest in electronics. Steve and his father would work together on electronics in the family garage. Steve's dad would show him how to take apart and reconstruct electronics, a hobby which built his confidence, tenacity and mechanical prowess.

As a young man, Steve was very intelligent, but formal schooling was just didn't work for him. In elementary school, he was a a bit a a problem causer and one of his teachers tried hard to bribe him to study. Steve's ability at test taking was so great that school administrators wanted to move him to high school, but his parents were against it.

While in high school, Steve met a new firned in the computer club named Steve Wozniak. The two of them began working to gether at Hewlett-Packard.

Steve actually dropped out of college after about six months. Formalized education just didn't work for Steve; however, he continued to educate himself informally and he continued to pursue his God-given passion for electronics. Eventually he and Wozniak were able to create their own company - Apple computers.

Steve's purpose and passion have changed the world's awareness of the design and functionality of electronics. The products Steve has designed are product people absolutely have to have, and once they have them they love them. In 2011 Forbes Apple was named the most valuable company in the world by Forbes magazine.

That very year Steve dies fromm complications resulting from pancreatic cancer, but his purpose and passion have changed our lives forever. He followed the path that *resonated* with him since his youth. He refused to allow success myths to force him down a dissonant path. Steve Jobs was not concerned about making a living. He was never concerned about "doing" what so-called "unsuccessful people" weren't willing to do, nor was he overly concerned about "the path of formal education." He had an "inside-out' focus and he was true to his innate gifts and talents. (http://en.wikipedia.org/wiki/Steve_jobs)

Carrie Wilkerson

Carrie Wilkerson's passion is being able to stay at home with her young children. Although she needed to provide income for her family, her inner-guidance led her to begin creating home-based businesses. In her new best-selling book, Barefoot Executive, she says: "I don't have a business degree. I've never taken a certified business class or been "credentialized" in any formal way. My advice is from real application, practical techniques, and solid experience. From babysitting and bagging groceries for tips, to being a barefoot CEO, we really are in a time when we can create our own realities. No longer do we rely on a standard track of education, then apply for a job, stay until we retire, and pray for security and good benefits along the way. We really are in a position to create our own careers, our own paths, and our own incomes, if we dare."[8]

It's important to follow your dreams and to let your children follow theirs. It's best that we not try to control them or persuade them to follow our dreams for them. We can help them see their gifts and talents, but let them find what resonates with them.

Susan Boyle

Another name many of us are familiar with is that of Susan Boyle. But many people aren't familiar with the story behind her success. Susan Boyle grew up in Scotland. She was the youngest of four brothers and five sisters. Complications at the time of her birth, caused her to have a learning disablitly and she was bullied throughout her years at school.

After leaving school, she was only able to work at menial jobs and but she did performed at many of local venues.

Susan actually won several singing competitions and her mother urged her to enter "Britain's Got Talent" competition. This would be the first time she had attempted to sing in front of an audience bigger than her church parish. Susan's singing coach said that Susan decided not to audition for The X Factor because she was afraid that people would only be chosen mainly for their looks.

She almost gave up on her decision to enter Britain's Got Talent because she believed she was too old, but her coach persuaded her to go ahead and give it a try. Susan later admitted that the number one thing inspiring her was an inner desire to honor her mother and her performance was the first time she had sung in public since her mother's death. Although she did pay tribute to her mother, she did not do it because it was her mother's dream for her. Her mother helped her see her gifts, but Susan followed what resonated for her.

In August 2008, she applied for an audition for "Britain's Got Talent." Out of 43,212 contestants, she was accepted after her first audition. When Susan came on stage, she opened up and confessed that her dream and her passion was to become a famous professional singer like Elaine Paige, which, of course, drew condescending snickers from the judges as well as the audience.

When Susan opened her mouth and began to sing, her performance was so powerful and moving that the judges' faces reflected complete shock and awe. Susan performed a breath-taking rendition of "I Dreamed a Dream" from Les Misérables. She had just performed in front of an audience of over 10 million viewers. Program judge, Amanda Holden, remarked that hearing Susan's performance was "the biggest wake-up call ever" for her.

Susan said, "I know what they were thinking, but why should it matter as long as I can sing? It's not a beauty contest."

This performance was widely reported and tens of millions of people viewed it on YouTube. Susan was astounded by this overwhelming reaction. After Susan;s appearance, Elaine Paige expressed an interest in singing with Boyle, stating that Susan is "a role model for everyone who has a dream". Boyle's rendition of "I Dreamed a Dream" has been credited with causing a surge in ticket sales in the Vancouver production of Les Misérables. Cameron Mackintosh, the producer of the Les Misérables musical, also praised the performance, as "heart-touching, thrilling and uplifting"

Boyle's first album, "I Dreamed a Dream," was released on 23 November 2009. In Britain, Boyle's debut album was recognized as the fastest selling UK debut album of all time selling 411,820 copies. In November 2010, Boyle became one of only three acts ever to top both the UK and US album charts twice in the same year. (http://en.wikipedia.org/wiki/Susan_boyle)

Susan Boyle had seeds of greatness within her. She had a dream that inspired her to take action, and thankfully her grades in school were no deterrence to her true success. Her true success flowed from who she was created to be. Your Divine Purpose is not only something you truly love doing. It is also something you are naturally gifted at. It is something you can share with the world in a positive way, while filling you with a sense of purpose and satisfaction. There may not always be formal education that is designed for your unique purpose. Follow your inner guidance and you will be led to everything you need to learn.

Myth #7 – Security Equals Success

"People are constantly seeking security, and you will find that seeking security is actually a very ephemeral thing. Even attachment to money is a sign of insecurity. You might say, 'When I have X million dollars, then I'll be secure. Then I'll be financially independent and I will retire. Then I will do all the things I really want to do.' But it never happens – never happens. Those who seek security chase it for a lifetime without ever finding it. It remains elusive and ephemeral, because security can never come from money alone. Attachment to money will always create insecurity no matter how much money you have in the bank."[9]

When you are living your passion and loving what you do, you no longer live for vacations. Retirement is no longer your focus, because your focus is on living today.

When you are aligned with Divine Purpose you are not waiting until age 65 to begin living your dreams and passions. A financial advisor recently told me that 95% of the U.S. population reaches retirement age without having accumulated a retirement income of $30,000 a year, in spite of deferring their dreams and passions for 40 years.

"You don't need to have a complete and rigid idea of what you'll be doing next week or next year because if you have a very clear idea of what's going to happen and you get rigidly attached to it, then you shut out a whole range of possibilities."[10]

The Children of Israel put their Divine Purpose, a Land of Promise, on hold for forty years while they walked in circles in a desert. Does that sound familiar? Their journey could have been completed in eleven days, but they wanted *certainty* over having to trust and believe. Their Promised Land was right there for them to possess, but their limited mindset made it hard to believe that God had a Divine Purpose for them. Instead of marching triumphantly in to claim it, they found themselves wandering in a wilderness for forty years. God finally called them to leave their limiting beliefs behind, by saying: "You have dwelt long enough on this mountain." (Deuteronomy 1:6) Their Divine Purpose, an abundant life in a Land of Promise, eluded them because limiting beliefs kept them dissonant to the "goodness of God."

True Success is not found in security, but in trusting that all you need will be provided when you align with your Divine Purpose.

Myth #8 – It's Too Late For Success

"It is never too late to be what you might have been."

– George Eliot

How often do we hear this, "If you haven't built your nest egg by the time you are 50 years old you are never going to retire." That myth does nothing but discourage people from excelling at a time in their lives when they have acquired great wisdom and experience. Many of society's most successful people were just beginning to make strides toward successes when they were 50.

If you have heard of the novel Ben Hur, you have heard of **Lew Wallace**. He was 53 years old when it became the best-selling novel in the 19th century. It has never been out of print.

Harlan David Sanders (Colonel Sanders) was 65 years old when he started Kentucky Fried Chicken. Kentucky Fried Chicken was a brand new business idea for him. In his youth, Sanders worked many different jobs from farming to steamboat pilot, to insurance salesman. When he turned 40 years old, he started a service station and sold chicken dinners to his patrons. Over a number of years he developed the way he pressure fried the chicken. As the demand for his special chicken grew, he opened a restaurant. As fate would have it, a major interstate was built, which diverted traffic away from the road his restaurant was on. Sanders decided to franchise his business and Kentucky Fried Chicken was born.

Ben Franklin was a late bloomer as well. He accomplished some great things early in life, but many of his greatest accomplishments came as he got older. It wasn't until he was 46 that he conducted his famous experiment with electricity and a kite. At 47, he won the Copley Award, an early version of the Nobel Prize. Between the ages of 47 and 49 he came up with some of his most notable inventions: bifocals, the catheter, and the Franklin Stove. It wasn't until he was 69 that he was finally elected to the Continental Congress. He was 70 when he signed the Declaration of Independence. When he was 77 years old, he negotiated the Treaty of Paris, which put an end to the Revolutionary War. And at the ripe old age of 81, he signed the U.S.Constitution.

Henry Ford introduced the Model T automobile when he was 45 years old. At the age of 60, he created the first car assembly line.

Soichiro Honda was 42 years old when he formed the Honda Motor Company in 1948. He created the motorbike by attaching a small engine to a bicycle This success led him to designing a small motorcycle and within 10 years of starting Honda, he was the leading motorcycle manufacturer in the world. He started manufacturing small engines and cars and the rest is history. In 1988, at the age of 82, he was the 1st Japanese automobile manufacturer to be included in the Automobile Hall of Fame.

Julia Child was 49 years old when her 1st cookbook "Mastering the Art of French Cooking," was published. At 51 years old she gained television fame with her cooking show, which premiered in 1963. At the age of 69, she became co-founder of the American Institute of Wine and Food to help advance the knowledge of food and wine through restaurants. In 1984, at the age of 72, she completed a series of 6 videotapes titled "The Way to Cook". (http://toknowinfo. hubpages.com/hub/Success-Stories-Never-Too-Old-Never-Too-Late-Late-Bloomers-Dreams-and-Achievements)

Myth # 9 – I'm Not worthy of Success

Your inner world shapes your outer world. If you don't fully believe in yourself, your brain won't be able to visualize your dreams or guide you to take inspired action. If you have any self-doubt, hidden fears or uncertainty, they will sabotage True Success.

"True success" is not merited. It is a gift that flows freely to you as you "hone-in" on your Higher Purpose.

There is nothing personal about the ways in which universal laws operate. The Universe doesn't check to see if you are worthy, or if are a good enough person. Your Divine Purpose was custom-made for you just the way you are. You don't need to worry about being "smart enough" or "good enough." The sooner you accept yourself just as you are, the sooner you will begin sending out a high-frequency signal that aligns with your Divine Purpose.

Universal laws reflect back into your life an exact match of the signal you are sending out. If you send out a signal of low self-worth, you will attract outcomes of the same frequency.

One thing that I've found that prevents many people from getting what they "say" they want is an underlying belief that tells them they are unworthy to actually have it. If you find that you are unable to make lots of money, it may be the thought held in the subconscious mind is something such as "I don't deserve to be prosperous." In order to change your beliefs, you have to operate at the level of the subconscious mind. You will need to re-write your subconscious blueprint to believe you deserve to have a wonderful life. I will address this in chapter 4. The truth is, we are all deserving of all good.

Whatever you focus your "*attention*" on grows stronger in your life, and your "*intention*" organizes its fulfillment. So focus your attention on the "goodness of your true self" and you will resonate with the "goodness of God."

When you are aligned with your "true self"- your spirit, you will experience your innate worth. Feelings of unworthiness result only as you deviate from that connection. God created your Divine Purpose because He knows your Divine-worth.

Feelings of unworthiness stem from an "outside-in" focus. They are ego-based! Ego tells you to compare yourself with others and makes you feel like you are separate from your Divine Source. As you resonate with your Higher Power you will experience an intimacy with your true self that brings healing.

Myth #10 – Success Has Limits

At a very young age many of us had the belief drilled into our heads that resources are scarce and limited, and that if you want something for yourself, you'll have to take it from someone else.

This creates the limiting belief that: "there is not enough abundance to go around." This is what Garrett Gunderson calls: "the myth of the finite pie." He says that: "Most of us think there is a finite resource "pie" from which we all share and that the more we have, the less others have, and vice versa[11] This myth keeps us from understanding that true success is possible for everyone because the Universe is infinitely abundant. Scarcity is only an illusion we create in our minds.

The more we share our Divine Purpose with others, the more value we create in their lives. The more value we give the more we receive in return. The wider we cast our seed, the greater the harvest! As you take the seed of your Divine Purpose and cast it as wide and as far as possible, you will be adding value to the lives of many people.

Myth #11: Money is the Root of All Evil

"Something is holy or unholy according to the purpose the mind ascribes to it. In the hands of fear, money can be harmful; in the hands of love, it can be healing and helpful."
– Marianne Williamson

This may be the most powerful myth of all, causing us to have prejudices and stereotypes about money that are at odds with our Divine Purpose. True Success opens the windows of heaven to abundance that flows from an infinitely abundant source. This way of looking at money actually keeps our highest good at bay.

By aligning our thoughts about money with the same spiritual truths that inform every other aspect of our lives, we are lifted to a realm of infinite abundance and ever increasing good.

As I have had the opportunity to talk with people about my journey, and tell them about the title for this book, they always ask me, **"How do I align with my Divine Purpose?"** It all starts with resonance, but there are other principles that make your transformation possible. The rest of this book is dedicated to answering that important question.

Jack Canfield said: "With a purpose, everything in life seems to fall into place. To be 'on purpose' means you're doing what you love to do, doing what you're good at and accomplishing what's important to you. When you truly are on purpose, the people, resources, and opportunities you need naturally gravitate toward you. The world benefits, too, because when you act in alignment with your true purpose, all your actions automatically serve others."[12]

Summary

How do I apply the principle of Resonance?

1. Make a commitment to do something that brings you joy every day. This helps you get in touch with your Divine Purpose.

2. Become aware of whether your current focus is "inside-out" or "outside-in."

3. Identify the myths or lies you have accepted as truth.

Benefits of applying Principle One

1. You will gain an understanding of how to begin aligning with True Success.

2. You will begin to rediscover what resonance feels like.

3. You will gain an understanding of how Universal Laws work in our lives

4. You will begin to experience effortless "flow."

5. You will identify the myths that have kept you dissonant from True Success.

Consequences of not applying Principle One

You'll be missing out on one of the most effective methods available to finally align with your dreams and implement real transformational change in your life

You will retain the same dissonance:

- Anxiety,
- Struggling with self-defeating behaviors or addictions,
- Depression,
- Remaining stuck in a job you hate,
- Making a living, but not living,
- Stuck at a certain level of income,
- Burned out,
- Unemployed or under-employed,
- Spiritually and emotionally empty
- Living without purpose
- Looking for an easier way
- Held back by a your level of education
- Struggling with limiting beliefs

1. **Principle One Exercise If time and money weren't an issue, and failure was a non-existent concept, what would you create? Why does the world need it?**

2. **As a child, what tasks did you complete successfully, with enjoyment? As an adult what do you do well?**

3. **What is something that you do regularly that you cannot imagine not doing?**

4. **When a friend is in need, what do you bring to them?**

5. **What is one topic of conversation that you could insert yourself into, and talk about for hours?**

6. When you lose track of time what are you doing?

7. What do you love so much that you would pay for the privilege of having it, or doing it?

8. What do you consistently receive compliments about? What do people consistently ask you to help them with? What do people flock to you for?

9. What are you consistently complaining about? What's the gap that you consistently notice?

   - Bonus – Go to my website www.PrinciplesofDivinePurpose.com and get FREE download

   - Bonus – Go to my website www.PrinciplesofDivinePurpose.com and get FREE videos

   - Bonus – Go to my website www.PrinciplesofDivinePurpose.com and get FREE coaching session.

   - Bonus – Go to my website www.PrinciplesofDivinePurpose.com and invite me to speak at your meeting

Workbook Exercises

- Focus on developing an awareness of your gifts, talents, dreams and passions.

- Focus on how these things cause you to experience feelings of *resonance* and if there are any feelings of *dissonance*. Write down a description of "Your Divine Purpose." (similar to a mission statement)

- Include a description of how it will impact and add value to the lives of other.

CHAPTER TWO

How to Access the "Flow" of True Success
Principle # 2: Universal Energy

"Everything is energy and that's all there is to it . . ."

– Albert Einstein

In order to understand the principles that will follow it is essential to have a firm grasp on principle number two – "everything is energy." I struggled with understanding and believing this concept at first. It just seemed too strange in the beginning. It required faith in something unseen that really wasn't a mainstream teaching that I was familiar with.

Science has shown that everything at its most basic level is energy, but applying that to success in my personal life didn't make sense.

If you are struggling with anything in your life - bad relationships, poor health, lack of financial abundance or a general sense of unhappiness, the root of your problem, challenge or sickness, lies at the energy level.

If there are barriers in any area of your life keeping you from the True Success you desire, there is resistance in your energy system.

As we move forward, I will often be using the word "frequency," so let me take a minute to describe it. One way to understand "frequency" is to imagine a room filled with people who are sharing love and joy with each other. This room has a feeling of lightness, a high frequency, whereas a room filled with angry, tense people has a feeling of heaviness - a low frequency.

As I began trying to apply Universal laws I continually slipped back into trying to make my own success happen, instead of allowing it to flow. The idea of "allowing" was completely foreign to me.

According to Christy Whitman, there are 7 Universal Laws that define how universal energy works in the process of creation.

1. **The Law of attraction** - The Law of Attraction states that the energy we broadcast out into the universe draws to itself energies that are of an equal frequency, resonance, or vibration.

2. **The Law of allowing** – which has to do with removing all resistance, noticing when you are feeling constricted, and allowing the flow of source energy.

3. **The Law of deliberate creation** – Which has to do with your

ability to create the life you desire by choosing your vibrational frequency.

4. **The Law of sufficiency and abundance** – Which has to do with the Universe having no shortage, lack or limitations. As you align your mind with abundance, your body actually vibrates in abundance.

5. **The Law of detachment** – teaches us to focus on our intention without the restriction of doubt, desperation or time frames.

6. **The Law of pure potentiality** – which has to do with the infinite potential for things to be created and manifested.

7. **The Law of polarity** – Which means there are polar opposites of everything that we focus on. This means whenever we think about anything that we desire - whether it's money, success, intimacy, fun, fulfillment - we are focused either on its presence, or on its absence.

Christy Whitman on the Inspiration show h[3]

Although it took a while I finally began to see that aligning with Divine Purpose brings access to a power far beyond our own. We gain access to the power by which the Universe operates, and the power by which worlds are created. This power is Universal energy.

As you progress through these principles you will come to see that when you get energy flowing in the direction you want it to go, life becomes effort-less, there is no longer any need for forcing or will-power.

What is flow?

It is a peaceful, calm and joyful state marked by the flow of inspiration and confidence. This would be your natural state without the existence of resistance (dissonance). This is the state I experienced as a child playing baseball. Flow brings a heightened sense of awareness and focus, because we are resonating with our divine gifts. In this state of mind, we are fully living in the present and there is no self-criticism. Because we are immersed in the here and now, our actions seem "effortless!" There is an increased belief that our dreams and goals can become realized. There is also a sense of deep enjoyment when we are in this unique, special and magical state of being.

Flow is a vibrational state of pure positive energy where all our hopes are held until we align with it. When we are close to it, we can feel its influence, and when we are not, we can feel that we are distanced from it.

In the competitive world in which we live, we are often faced with pressure to perform to our fullest potential. It is easier to manage these challenges if we know how take charge of our thoughts and emotions in ways that can assist us in accessing a flow state.

Methods for "getting in the zone" have been used by top athletes from virtually every sport you can think of. However, accessing a flow state is not just for world class athletes. These methods are also widely used by executives, attorneys, chief executive officers, stay at home moms and by students who want to perform well on demanding exams. Anyone who wants True Success can benefit from learning how to get into "the zone."

If you are nervous, self-critical or not living in the present, you will find it very difficult to experience flow.

Flow is a resistance-free connection to our True Self. We get into the flow by eliminating the resistance that keeps us from it. It's only when we have more resistance than belief that we can be kept out.

To understand this amazing state we need to learn more about an unseen power called Universal Energy or Source Energy, and how to connect to it. I believe this type of connection is what people are really seeking for when they turn to self-help and personal development. Connection with Source Energy is a connection to True Self, True Success and Divine Purpose!

This type of connection is not accomplished with an "outside-in" focus. It is not accomplished by ego, willpower, or self-discipline. If you don't like a movie, you don't go to the screen to try to change it. You go to the projection booth and put in another film. In the same way, flow is accomplished at a spiritual-energy level, by means of divinely created Universal Laws. It requires Divine Power that brings about a fundamental change in our energy makeup. This type of transformation requires a "mighty change" in our vibrational signal.

Everything is Energy

"Everything is energy and that's all there is to it. Match the frequency of the reality you want and you cannot help but get that reality. It can be no other way. This is not philosophy; this is science."

– Albert Einstein

It's not Philosophy; it's Science

I love that Einstein said; "this is not philosophy; this is science," but maybe he could have said "It's not just philosophy, it's also science," because I believe it is both. I believe Einstein found the connection between philosophy and science. It's called Universal law!

Universal laws are where science and philosophy come together; it is where the physical *(visible)* and *spiritual (invisible)* worlds combine. Einstein's statement that "everything is made up of unseen energy," helps connect True Success with Divine Purpose.

All physical matter is just energy vibrating at different frequencies. This is a universal law that has been confirmed by science. Spiritual matter is energy as well; it just vibrates at a much higher frequency.

In order to access the higher frequency of the spiritual realm, you must raise your own frequency. There are numerous things you can do to raise your frequency. First, though, you must truly have the intent to learn with spiritual guidance about loving yourself and others. When you have a true, pure intent to learn, your frequency automatically rises. Your intent to learn is your most powerful tool for raising your frequency.

I believe that part of Albert Einstein's Divine Purpose was to discover that "everything is energy." Your beliefs, your thoughts, your emotions are made up of energy that affects your ability to resonate with the right people, opportunities and inspired ideas. Your Divine Purpose has a vibrational frequency that flows from a divine energy source. The frequency of that higher energy has the power to transform your life.

All Energy Flows From a Source of Divine Intelligence

Max Plank, another world renowned scientist, is known for his breakthroughs in the understanding of the atom. Scientists like Max are typically left-brained guys, who don't tend to be philosophical. By nature they need to have data and hard proof.

Amazingly, Max Plank, as he accepted the Nobel Prize, said: "As a man who has devoted his whole life to the most clear-headed science, to the study of matter, I can tell you, as the result of my research about Atoms, this much. There is no matter as such. All matter originates and exists only by virtue of a force which brings the particles of an Atom to vibration and holds this most minute solar system of the atom together."

The greatest scientist on the planet says: "We must assume that beyond this force is the existence of a conscious and intelligent mind. This mind is the matrix of all matter." – Max Plank.

It seems that the greatest scientific mind of our time is saying. There is a Source of intelligence from which all energy and power flow.

The Universe is God's Divinely Organized System

*"The whole universe, in its essential nature, is
the movement of energy and information."*
— Deepak Chopra

Whether we recognize it or not, universal physical laws like gravity are constantly at work in our lives. For instance, when an airplane is flying it would appear that the Law of Gravity is not in effect, but in reality it's because the Law of Gravity is in effect that the plane is actually able to fly. A plane cannot take off, steer, or maneuver without the power of gravity. Gravity is working in every aspect of flight.

Just as the Universe has constant physical laws, like the law of gravity, it also has spiritual laws which work nonstop and affect all aspects of our lives. These laws exist in The Universe as part of God's divinely organized system by which all things operate.

Energy is a part of this divinely organized system. It makes up the building blocks out of which the universe constructs every material thing, including all forms of life. Through a process which only Divine Intelligence completely understands, the universe translates energy into matter. Nature's building blocks are available to man, in the energy involved in thinking! Napoleon Hill put it this way: "Man's brain may be compared to an electric battery. It absorbs energy from the ether, which permeates every atom of matter, and fills the entire universe."[14] When you look at your hand it appears to be solid, but it isn't. Solidity is actually a mirage. If you could look at it through a powerful microscope you would see it as a mass of energy vibrating at very high speeds. The reason your hand feels solid is because of the rate at which the energy is vibrating. Everything you observe with your physical senses is vibrational interpretation. You hear because your ears translate vibration. You see because your eyes translate vibration.

All of your senses are about the translation of vibration. However, our physical senses cannot tell us the whole truth. For example, the frequency of a dog whistle is dissonant, or imperceptible to our ears, yet its frequency resonates very perceptibly for dogs.

Human beings are also frequency generators. We now have machines that can actually measure the energy that a person's brain is giving off. The most potent form of energy is thought. As difficult as it is to comprehend, our thoughts penetrate all space and all time, and every thought has its own frequency. If we continuously focus on a certain thought, we emit that frequency on a continuous basis.

A very well-known and well-documented example of this universal law is the placebo effect, which is used in medication trials. Even the most carefully designed double-blinded study almost always yields very measurable placebo improvement. Patients who believed they would be affected positively by the medications fared better than those who did not, even when given an inert tablet (often a sugar pill). This is because the frequency of their beliefs is resonating with the Source of healing power.

In the age of modern-day electronics, it's easier to comprehend universal laws and unseen energy frequencies. Just as we can connect instantly to information through the power of the internet, we also connect to unseen energy frequencies by means of our thoughts and emotions.

The Source of True Success
Source Energy Flows From Its Creator

There is an energy field that is constantly at work in our lives. This energy flows from the presence of a Divine creator and fills the immensity of space. This energy is the light by which all things are governed, it gives life to all things, and it is the source from which True Success - Divine Purpose flows.

This is an email I recently received titled "A Letter from God, (or the Universe)" I adapted it a little:

"Remember, you are not average! Your fingerprints are different from anyone else's on this earth. You are a unique combination of DNA that has never been, and will never be seen again in the world. While you're here, choose to align with your Divine Purpose, find out what you love to do most, and do it. If you do that, I will literally shower you with success."

Resonance with Source Energy requires a high vibrational frequency. If our beliefs, thoughts and emotions are broadcasting a low-vibrational signal, that resonance cannot take place, it goes against Universal law.

In the Old Testament, David wrote: "surely goodness and mercy shall follow me all the days of my life. Notice, he was expecting goodness and mercy, not part of the time, but all the days of his life. The Message translation puts it this way: "God's kindness and goodness chases me down everywhere I go." David's attitude was, "I just can't get away from the goodness of God!" **Source energy is the grace of God!** It is the *divine help* and *enabling power* that flow from Him**.**

Jennifer Vasilakos

Recently I read an article about a woman, who through her faith was able to quickly receive the "flow" of blessings she desired. We sometimes refer to these types of experiences as miracles, but in reality they are Universal laws at work. The headline read: "A woman who helped a lost man ended up with a surprise $20,000 gift."

That's what happened last month when Jennifer Vasilakos helped Ty Warner when he stopped to ask for driving directions in Santa Barbara, Calif.

While Warner didn't know exactly how to get to where he was going, Vasilakos didn't realize who she was helping. Warner is the billionaire founder of Ty Inc., the Beanie Baby company.

Vasilakos was at the intersection trying to raise $20,000 for a stem cell procedure she needs to help save her life because she suffers from kidney failure and does not qualify for a transplant.

This is her description from her blog:

I often get asked by random strangers for directions. Not one to miss an opportunity, I handed him my flyer and he made a fifty dollar donation. As he drove off, I thought that was the end of our encounter... He'd returned after an hour or so. Rolling down his window, he reached out his hand and introduced himself. I immediately recognized his name. He was kind and sincere as he looked directly into my eyes... I listened as he repeated over and over that he was going to help me - that my fundraising was done – that I didn't need to worry any longer. He said he would send a check after he returned to his offices during the week.

He was true to his word. Vasilakos, an herbalist and Reiki teacher, received a package on July 16 with a $20,000 check and with a handwritten note from Warner. The note read in part, "Someone up there loves you because I was guided to meet you Saturday. I never lose my way, but fate had me lost and ask you for directions. The rest of the story I hope will be a wonderful new life for you."

"Of course I started crying, because that's what girls do," Vasilakos said. "I'm incredibly thankful to Ty Warner and to everyone who has supported me with love and prayer."

The check cleared a few weeks later and she booked a surgical procedure at an undisclosed foreign hospital to begin hematopoietic stem cell treatment. Hematopietic treatment takes a cell from the blood or bone marrow that can renew itself and develop into a variety of specialized cells.

"After I serendipitously met Jennifer, I further educated myself on her stem cell needs. I was shocked that this particular type of treatment wasn't available to her in the U.S.," Warner said in a media release. "My hope is that we can bring this lifesaving treatment to the forefront so that it can become more readily available and provide alternatives for people like Jennifer."

So the chance meeting allowed both Warner and Vasilakos to each continue on their journeys.

Was it just a coincidence that Ty Warner came by at exactly the right time, or was it Universal law at work, connecting her faith to her Divine Source. (http://www.huffingtonpost.com/2012/08/23/ty-warner-beanie-baby-billionaire_n_1826320.html)

We could say that the goodness that flows from God is that Source Energy that chases us down everywhere we go because it is an unseen yet omnipresent spiritual energy. This energy surrounds us constantly, and just like radio waves it remains undetected unless we tune into its frequency. Our Divine Purpose flows from this source of energy.

On summer evenings, I occasionally sit in my front yard watching the sun's light as it hits the spray of water from my sprinklers. When this happens a beautiful rainbow of colors can be seen as the sun's light is refracted. It is a marvel to me how these previously invisible colors suddenly appear when light is refracted.

We could refer to Source Energy as spiritual "light," because of the frequency at which it vibrates. Just like physical light, spiritual light contains an invisible rainbow of spiritual elements: things like charity, abundance, inspiration, creativity, and expansiveness.

Ralph Waldo Emerson was quoted as saying: *"Most of the shadows of life are caused by standing in our own sunshine."*

Source energy, Divine Intelligence or spiritual light, operates at a much higher frequency than physical energy. We could say that the *"goodness of God"* is light that fills the immensity of space.

Because it is spiritual in nature its source is pure goodness and well-being. This divine energy provides for all our needs, it contains infinite information and contains the answer to every question. Because spiritual frequencies are dissonant to our physical senses it is easy to discount their reality.

There is a constant flow of grace flowing from the source of Divine energy. We can compare Source Energy to the light of the Sun. The light contains everything we need and desire in abundance, and it shines on each of us the same. It is up to us to choose whether we will hide in a dark basement, carry around a sun umbrella, or bask in the warmth of its rays, but light does not discriminate.

It is the energy of our beliefs, thoughts and emotions that determine the amount of Divine light we allow into our lives. If we desire an abundant life, we must allow ourselves to be filled with abundant light.

Source is An Unseen Energy Field

We live in a time where we now have physical evidence of things in the unseen realm. We have the technology today that allows us to see the patterns created by sound waves as they pass through water and other mediums. We can actually see the patterns change and become more detailed as the frequency is raised or lowered. We have technology to see the patterns created by the frequency of a singer's voice. We have the technology to see a person's brain waves. We can freeze water into crystals and see the patterns that were created by the frequencies of music, words and even emotions.

We live in a day when we can push the power button on our remote control and see a picture appear on our TV screen. Even though we cannot see the signals traveling through the air, we now have evidence of their existence. In a way, we are like a television. As we choose our beliefs, thoughts and emotions we are transmitting an energy signal. The frequency of our signal determines the energy we will attract back into our lives. Is your signal attracting the realization of your dreams and passions? Is your signal one of faith and expectancy, or one of fear and doubt?

Faith is Energy!
Faith is a Substance

We are human transmission towers, transmitting a frequency with our thoughts and feelings. We can change anything in our lives by changing the frequency of our thoughts.

We are all affected by this unseen power called energy! Biblical teachings say that unseen things are only comprehended by faith. Paul taught the Hebrews that: "Faith is the **substance** of things hoped for, the evidence of things not seen." (Heb 11:1) Faith is energy that resonates with its Source (the Power of God).

Notice, faith has to do with the unseen world – the spiritual world. What Paul might have been trying to say is that, faith is an actual unseen substance, or we could say that, faith is actually an unseen **energy,** with the power (or frequency) to connect us to the things we hope for, but cannot see.

Faith is High-Frequency Energy

Faith is spiritual energy that resonates with the energy of our Divine Purpose. Resonance is evidence that our Divine Purpose is assisting us to expand our vision and conceive of what's possible in our lives. Our Divine Purpose is like a seed that needs to take root. If it is nurtured and cared for with the energy of faith, it brings forth good fruit – an abundant life of True Success!. The *Law of faith* requires that we place our trust in God (our Divine Source) that our purpose will manifest in divine timing.

In each of our lives there is resistance that keeps us from possessing what our Divine Purpose has in store. We have two choices: we can give up and live in mediocrity, or we can take hold of victory. Remember, it is only when we have more resistance than we do belief that we are kept from the flow of our Divine Purpose. In scriptural terms, we could say our Divine Purpose is our Promised Land.

In the Old Testament, the children of Israel were camped right next door to their Promised Land. God had already told them He would give them the victory; all they had to do was enter the land and fight. But, when they experienced the resistance of their opponent's physical size, their weak and defeated mentality led them to give up. Their attitude was, "What's the use of even trying? We'll never defeat those people. We might as well just stay out here in the wilderness." They settled for mediocrity because they weren't willing to fight.

The battle we all fight is in our minds. We have to change our thinking in order to possess the promises of our Divine Purpose. We can choose thoughts of faith and victory. We can declare that we are overcomers. As we stand and fight and win the battle in our mind, we'll move forward and embrace the promises and dreams that the "goodness of God" has for us!

The Bible says: "In God's strength I can do all things." This is what Divine Purpose means! It means setting aside self-sufficiency or ego and aligning with an energy source that is infinite. When we are in a vibrational alignment with the flow of Divine inspiration, we can indeed do all things.

David understood this principle when he faced Goliath. He wasn't concerned with how big Goliath was. Instead he was focused on the infinite "goodness of God." What do you focus on when you're faced with your own Goliaths? What about when you're faced with the size of a big dream? Never give up on a dream just because of the time it will take to accomplish it. The time will pass anyway. Never talk fear, talk faith!

When you're in an attitude of faith, the "goodness of God" resonates in your life and works for you in whatever your situation.

Peter, the Apostle of Jesus Christ, being full of the energy of faith, was able to walk on water. The energy of the faith that flowed through him, made his physical body resonate with the energy of the water, allowing him to walk upon it. It was only when he allowed fear and doubt to enter his thoughts that he began to sink. We would call this a miracle, but it is just a higher manifestation of Universal Law.

You may be struggling financially, in all kinds of debt, but your Divine Purpose is telling you "now is the time for freedom." You may be bound by addictions and bad habits, but your Divine Purpose is saying, "It's time to step into victory." You may have been burdened with bad health, but Divine Purpose is saying "now is the time for vibrant health." The Source Energy flows from God and contains all that is necessary for well-being, but you must change your own energy signal in order for it to flow.

As you align with Divine Purpose, you will experience victory in your life. Divine favor will be poured out in great measure.

There is a creator, and the goodness that emanates from Him is a powerful spiritual energy. This energy field is the source of all goodness, abundance, love, creativity and well-being. This energy field is "the goodness of God (or God's grace)."

Everything is energy! Scientists have proven that there is no such thing as matter – only energy vibrating at various frequencies. Our problems such as addictions, hate, war, cruelty, dishonesty and scarcity, are the result of a separation from Source Energy, (the goodness of God) and Divine Purpose

Faith Resonates with Source Energy

With God nothing is impossible, and as you connect to the energy that flows from His presence you are aligned with your Divine Purpose. It is when your connection to Source Energy becomes corroded that worldly concerns and problems take over. This energy field contains the divine help and abundance intended for a victorious and abundant life.

Whatever you truly desire to produce in life, it is not your ego that is going to produce it. It is your connection to Divine help – your Higher Power!

Miracles are Unseen Energy at Work

*"Miracles will be commonplace as you follow
your Higher Purpose"*

– Randall Brown

In the New Testament there is a fascinating account of two blind men who heard Jesus was passing by, and faith began to rise in their hearts. They cried out, "Jesus, Son of David, have mercy on us and heal us."

When Jesus heard their cries he asked a very important question. "Do you believe I am able to do this?" He wanted to know if they had real faith. The blind men answered back with assurance. They said, "Yes Lord; we believe. We know beyond a shadow of a doubt that you can heal us. We know you are able. We have trust and confidence in you." (Math 9:27-29)

When Jesus recognized their faith, he touched their eyes and said unto them, "According to your faith be it unto you." Their eyes were immediately opened. They believed God could do something great in their lives and they were healed.

It was the power of faith that made it all possible! The energy of their belief resonated with the "goodness of God" and resulted in the flow of healing energy.

Faith is an energy that operates by universal laws, unseen by our physical eyes. By exercising faith, these universal laws, as real as the law of gravity, will manifest Divine Purpose into our physical reality.

Faith itself is energy. What emotions do you experience when you are full of faith? What are your thoughts like? In this inspired state, doubt and lack don't seem to exist.

When you decide to exercise faith in something, you don't need to know how it is going to happen it will be shown to you. Inspiration will lead you as your high-frequency signal resonates with your Divine Purpose. This is the "evidence of things not seen" that Paul referred to.

Beliefs are Energy!

> *"You are what you are today because of what you believed about yourself yesterday, and tomorrow you will be what you believed about yourself today."*-
>
> Unknown

Story of Nick

Nick was a big strong man who worked in the railroad yards for many years, but he was known for having a chronically negative attitude. He seemed to always fear the worst and was constantly worried.

"One summer day, the crews were told that they could go home an hour early to celebrate the birthday of one of the foremen. All the workers left, but somehow Nick accidently locked himself in a refrigerated boxcar that had been brought into the yard for maintenance. The boxcar was empty and not connected to any of the trains.

When Nick realized that he was locked inside the refrigerated boxcar, he panicked. Nick began beating on the doors so hard that his arms and fists became bloody. He screamed and screamed, but his coworkers had already gone home to get ready for the party. Nobody could hear Nick's desperate calls for help. Again and again he called out, until finally his voice was a raspy whisper.

Aware that he was in a refrigerated boxcar, Nick guessed that the temperature in the unit was well below freezing, maybe as low as five or ten degrees Fahrenheit. Nick feared the worst. He thought, what am I going to do? If I don't get out of here, I'm going to freeze to death. There's no way I can stay in here all night. The more he thought about his circumstances, the colder he became. With the door shut tightly, and no apparent way of escape, he sat down to await his inevitable death by freezing or suffocation, whichever came first.

To pass the time, he decided to chronicle his demise. He found a pen in his shirt pocket and noticed an old piece of cardboard in the corner of the car. Shivering almost uncontrollably, he scribbled a message to his family. In it Nick noted his dire prospects: "Getting so cold. Body numb. If I don't get out soon, these will probably be my last words."

And they were.

The next morning, when the crews came back to work, they opened the boxcar and found Nick's body crumpled over in the corner. When the autopsy was completed, it revealed that Nick had indeed frozen to death.

Now, here's the fascinating enigma: the investigators discovered that the refrigeration unit for the car in which Nick had been trapped was not even on! In fact, it had been out of order for some time and was not functioning at the time of the man's death. The temperature in the car that night – the night Nick froze to death – was sixty-one degrees. Nick froze to death in slightly less than normal room temperatures because he believed that he was in a freezing boxcar. He expected to die! He was convinced that he didn't have a chance. He expected the worst. He saw himself as doomed with no way out. He lost the battle in his own mind[15]. Nick attracted what he believed. That seems to be evidence of the saying: "As a man thinketh in his heart, so is he." (Proverbs 23:7)

You cannot align with Divine Purpose, or experience the "goodness of God," until you choose to believe in success, victory, and progress. Cast away all negativity, cast away any thoughts that bring fear, worry, doubt, or unbelief. Your attitude should be: I refuse to go backward. I am going forward with the "goodness of God." I'm going to align with my Divine purpose.

If you do that the "goodness of God" will be activated in your life. You'll attract the solutions to your challenges. You'll have peace in the midst of any storm.

So what happens when you try to exercise faith but your subconscious mind says, "Yeah right?"

If this is your current reality, the limiting beliefs in your subconscious mind are sending a dissonant signal. In principle four we will learn how to reprogram and reframe limiting beliefs, but for now let's focus on understanding and believing in the reality of this unseen energy and how it operates by universal laws.

Believe in More than Your Eyes Can See!

Jack Canfield refused to believe only in what he was seeing in his current reality. As he began the process of finding a publisher, for what eventually became his best-selling book - "Chicken Soup for the Soul," he was rejected by 144 publishers, over the course of a two year span.

The publishers would say things like: "No one reads short stories, it's too positive, it's too nicey-nicey, it's not edgy enough, you're an unknown, you have no platform, you're not on Opera."

Jack eventually went to New York with his agent to try and connect with a publisher, after six days of trying, his agent finally gave him back his manuscript and said: "We can't sell it!"

Unwilling to give up, Jack attended the American Book Sellers Association convention in Anaheim, California, where he went from booth to booth for three days saying: "Will you read this book, will you publish this book, will you take a look at my book?" All he heard for three days was, "No, no, no, no," but late on the third day a little publisher from Florida said: "We'll take a copy and read it."

Two weeks later they called him back and said: "We love your book. We're going to publish it!" Jack said: "Great! Do we get an advance?" They quickly responded: "No, we don't give advances."

Jack then asked them: "How many copies do you expect to sell?" They said "twenty thousand." Jack replied: "That's not our vision!" The publisher asked: "What's your vision?" Jack said: "We want to sell one hundred and fifty thousand by Christmas. Then we want to sell a million and a half copies within a year and a half."

Have you ever shared your dream with someone and had them laugh out loud at you? Jack said: "My publisher laughed out loud!

The publisher said: "You guys are crazy!" But Jack replied: "No, we're entrepreneurs. We believe we can do this. We have a passion, a mission and a purpose. We feel divinely inspired!

Jack was in tune with the principle of resonance. He said "I couldn't get it out of my head." When asked later what kept him going after being rejected over a hundred times, he replied: "It was a divine obsession!" He went on to say: "I was guided to do this. I had to do this. I didn't have a choice." He knew in his heart that the rejections were not consistent with the resonance he felt.

Many people's beliefs are limited to what they see as their current reality, instead of allowing them to visualize the reality they truly desire. Because they can't imagine the possibility of great things happening in their lives, they accept their current reality as their truth. This is what is called a blind spot or a scotoma.

True Success comes to those who become success conscious and failure comes to those who become failure conscious.

Old Testament prophet Abraham, "Staggered not at the promise through unbelief, but was strong in faith; and being fully persuaded that, what he (God) had promised, he was able to perform." (Romans 4:20-21)

Abraham was promised a posterity as numerous as the stars of the sky and the sands of the sea, yet he had no offspring. He persisted in his faith until the promise was fulfilled even when there was no evidence in the physical realm.

Do you stagger at the promises of a Divine Purpose? Do you stagger to imagine True Success in your life because you see no evidence of it? Just because you can't see it doesn't mean it's not right there. There is a reason why you're not seeing it. It has to do with limiting beliefs that have been programed into your subconscious mind. We'll discuss techniques for changing this programing in a later chapter. But for now understand that the energy of your unbelieving thoughts is attracting only what appears to be possible.

Your personal vibrational energy, which you can control with your brain and thought patterns, is irresistibly attractive to anything else with a similar vibration.

Thoughts are Energy!

> *"You are what you think, not what you think you are"*
>
> – Bruce Maclelland

Scientists have proven that your thoughts travel 930,000 times faster than the speed of your voice. No other force or power in the Universe is known to be as great or as quick.

All thoughts are energy, and all thoughts and feelings have their own vibrational frequency. This means that every thought has a unique blueprint a little like a snowflake.

Every time we send one of these snowflakes out into the universe, it is received as an intention. The universe reflects back into our lives a vibrational match for our intentions. It is our dominant thought, or the thought that we dwell on most frequently, that creates the conditions of our life, even if it is subconscious! It doesn't matter what our other thoughts are, it is our dominant thought that affects our reality. This constant state of mind transmits an emotional signal that either resonates with our conscious desire or is dissonant from it.

How to Experience the Energy of Thoughts

Here is an exercise that will help you experience the energy of thoughts, try this experiment: Grab a notebook and pen and write the name of a person or thing that makes you feel good. Then start writing as many positive aspects of that thing that you can think of. Try to fill the entire page if you can. Then sit back and read what you wrote. You should notice that you feel light and uplifted afterwards. Do this for a few minutes every day, and you'll be amazed at how well it boosts your frequency and allows great things into your life!

If you will change your thinking, it will transform your energy. If you go around thinking thoughts of defeat and failure you cannot expect the "goodness of God" to fill you with joy, power, and victory. Thoughts of poverty and lack cannot resonate with abundance. The two concepts are incompatible."

You Get What You Think About – Period!

Napoleon Hill, the famous author of "Think and Grown Rich" once said: "More gold has been mined from the brains of men than has ever been taken from the earth." You get what you focus on. Your thoughts about your purpose are your purpose.

Robert Kiyosaki had a great observation about the title of Napoleon Hills book "Think and Grow Rich," He said: "There is a good reason why it's titled 'THINK and Grow Rich' and not Work Hard and Grow Rich, or Get a Job and Grow Rich…It's not what you have to 'do' that needs to change", expounds Kiyosaki, "It's first how you "think" that needs to change. In other words, it's who you have to 'be' in order to 'do' what needs to be done. … it's not the diet that counts; it's who you have to be to follow the diet that counts … A diet will not help if your thoughts do not change. (⁶

When the Apostle Paul said: "Faith is the substance of things hoped for, the evidence of things not seen," (Heb 11:1) I believe he was describing a *substance* from which everything in the universe is created. "To think a thought is an act of creation. If we clothe this thought in feeling, activate it with a strong desire to have it become manifest, the thought or idea begins to take form, to grow like a seed, to attract to itself the conditions, opportunities, resources and all the events necessary to enable its reproduction in our so-called material world." - Harold Sherman

If you want to live a life of abundance and financial prosperity, the first thing you need to do is start thinking like a person who is living that type of life. Your mental state and the composition of your thoughts should match the way you would think if you're already living your dream life.

Thoughts Have Creative Power

So what are you creating with your thoughts? If every thought you have says "I can't do this," nothing will be created. If on the other hand your thoughts are saying "I can do this," you are accessing the substance from which True Success will spring.

In his book The Holographic Universe, author Michael Talbot writes, " . . . Our hopes, fears, plans, worries, guilts, dreams and imaginings do not vanish after leaving our mind, but are turned into thought forms . . ."

Everything you focus on for more than a few minutes is being conceived as a possible manifestation in your life. A "thought form" is a manifestation of mental and emotional energy. When you focus on a thought consistently and you infuse it with strong emotional energy, you get a "thought form." A thought form is one step removed from a physical manifestation.

Here's a good way to think of it:

- A thought is the conception of a manifestation.
- A thought form is the gestation of a manifestation.
- The physical manifestation is the birth itself.

In Napoleon Hill's book "Think and Grow Rich," he discusses the importance of controlling one's own thoughts in order to achieve success, as well as the energy that thoughts have and their ability to attract other thoughts.

Too many people spend energy focusing on their problems. Because like-energies attract, focusing on what you don't want brings about more of what you don't want. What you think about you bring about. Fortunately, an affirmative thought is a hundred times more powerful than a negative thought. Your thoughts and your feelings create your life!

Because the energy of your thoughts is magnetic, that energy attracts situations and experiences of like-frequency. You think…you feel…you attract.

"Your dominant thoughts trigger a feeling within you, and that feeling emits a frequency that you broadcast out to the universe.

So how do we change our vibrational signal? The best way is to change our actual thoughts and thought patterns so they match the thoughts of those who already have achieved what we want to achieve; men like Napoleon Hill and Earl Nightengale.

Thoughts Are Things

> *"No thought stands still — it either takes you towards where you want to go or away from where you want to go."*
>
> – Andy Shaw

Napoleon Hill said: "Truly, "thoughts are things," and powerful things at that, when they are mixed with definiteness of purpose, persistence and a burning desire for their translation into riches or other material objects."[17]

An individual with desire, faith, and persistence can reach great heights by eliminating all negative energy and thoughts and focusing on the greater goals in hand.

Earl Nightengale explained the concept this way: "I'll tell you how it works, as far as we know. To do this, I want to tell you about a situation that parallels the human mind.

Suppose a farmer has some land, and it's good, fertile land. The land gives the farmer a choice; he may plant in that land whatever he chooses. The land doesn't care. It's up to the farmer to make the decision. We're comparing the human mind with the land because the mind, like the land. Doesn't care what you plant in it. It will return what you plant.

Now, let's say that the farmer has two seeds in his hand – one is a seed of corn, the other is nightshade, a deadly poison. He digs two little holes in the earth and he plants both seeds – one corn, the other night shade. He covers up the holes, waters and takes care of the land . . .and what will happen? Invariably, the land will return what was planted. As it's written in the Bible, "As ye sow, so shall ye reap". . .The human mind is far more fertile, far more incredible and mysterious than the land, but it works the same way. It doesn't care what we plant . . .success . . .or failure . . . You see, the human mind is the last great, unexplored continent on earth. It contains riches beyond our wildest dreams. It will return anything we want to plant."[18] Think from the end. See yourself already connected to what you want. You don't need to see the entire journey. When you're on a trip driving at night, you can only see about 100 yards in front of you, as far as the headlights go, then you go the next 100 yards and eventually you get there. When you use a GPS system you just follow the first set of instructions and the next and then the next until you finally arrive at your destination. It is the same with our goals. Our subconscious mind has its own GPS system and it finds the way. You don't have to know the whole way. You just start and go as far as you know and then the next part of the journey will come to you. Input the destination correctly and let the subconscious mind fill in the rest.

The correct way to put in the destination is to have a clear picture of what the destination looks like. It's like a smart bomb that is programed to hit its target. With the help of a satellite, it just keeps correcting until it finds the destination that's been programed in.

Researchers have found that new neural pathways can be created in 30-60 days with focused effort..[9] Once you do that something shifts in the brain. You'll start getting creative ideas as to how to reach your desired destination. You'll start seeing things you did not see before. You will experience a level of resonance that enables you to connect with your dreams. The interesting thing is that these resources are always there, we just don't see them because we are not resonating with them!.

Intentions Are Energy

"The most fulfilled people in any profession, regardless of who climbs to the top, are those who followed an inner vision . . . The externals of your life fall in line with your internal values and the atmosphere you create around yourself."
– Deepak Chopra

When Jack Canfield began working for W. Clement Stone, he was only making $8,000 a year. Because of the things Mr. Stone taught him about the power of intention, within a year Jack's income had increased to over $93,000. The power of intention is the power by which we can manifest our dreams and passions by developing beliefs, thoughts and emotions that resonate with our conscious desires.

When Jack was interviewing people for one of his books, he Interviewed Lou Holtz, the legendary Notre Dame Football coach. At the time Lou had just lost a head coaching job and was feeling discouraged and depressed. After his wife had gone back to work to help with the family finances, she came across a book that she gave Lou titled, "The Magic of Thinking Big." The book recommended creating 100 goals you want to accomplish in your life. Lou actually came up with 107 goals, including things like, winning a national championship, meeting the pope, etc. When he shared his list of goals with his wife, she commented: "you need another goal - find a job!" Lou quickly added that to his list of goals bringing the total to 108.

At the time Jack interviewed him, Lou had accomplished 102 of the goals on his list.

Intention requires writing down and getting clear on exactly what you want to attract into your life, what you want to be, do and have. A clear request is more likely to stimulate intense emotion.

Don't worry about "how" you're going to do something, just commit yourself to the end result and the way will be shown to you. Ask and believe, then you can receive. This eliminates the fear of failure.

For instance, if you want to go to medical school you don't eliminate it from your realm of possibility just because you don't have the money. You put it down as your intention, then you ask, you believe and you allow the way to be provided.

When I made it my intention to write a best-selling book, I knew I needed the expert help of marketing specialists, so I asked for help from people, God and the Universe - through my intentions. I believed help was coming and within a short time I received an email from a man named Steve Harrison. I participated in a few of his webinars and was very impressed with his ability to help author's get the publicity they need to become best-selling authors. I learned of his "Quantum Leap" coaching program and it resonated as part of my Divine Purpose. The problem was that I didn't have the money to pay for the program. So again, I asked in the same way, and within a few days, I had received the funding to enroll in the program.

If your Divine Purpose is calling, don't let a lack of anything keep you from it! Create your intention by asking and believing, then allow what is needed to manifest. The power (or energy) of your intention will draw it into your life through the Universal Law of Attraction.

Emotions are energy!

"Emotions are the language the Universe understands"

> – Unknown

The home team advantage

A number of years ago my favorite college football team was playing the number one team in the country. They were significantly out-matched in talent and athleticism, but they were playing at home in front of a very large and supportive home crowd. Fortunately, my team got off to a good start and the response of the crowd was electrifying. It quickly became evident that the energy of the crowd was creating unbelievable momentum. This momentum continued and to my amazement it actually heightened as the game went on. As the game ended, my underdog team came away with the biggest victory in school history, and it took a few days for the fans to recover.

This, to me, was evidence that *emotions are energy.* The advantage that the home team has in a sporting event is amazing. Why does this advantage exist? The playing fields (or courts) are the same size, the rules are the same, and they use the same equipment.

The energy generated by the fans greatly affects the thought patterns, and emotional states of the players they are supporting. If you look at a team's statistics over the course of a season, it's clear to see that teams perform significantly better at home. This is evidence of Universal laws at work!

"The Universe corresponds to the nature of your song."

"The mass of men lead lives of quiet desperation
and go to the grave with the song still in them."
-Henry David Thoreau

One of my favorite hymns is "Come Thou Fount of Every Blessing" by Robert Robinson. Robinson must have experienced powerful resonance as he wrote these inspired words:

"Come thou fount of every blessing *tune my heart* to sing thy grace."

There is a *fount* from which all goodness flows, an energy source called "the goodness of God." If our hearts, or our emotions, are "tuned" to sing in *harmony* with God's goodness, the universe will correspond to the nature of our song. As our emotions transmit God-like, high-energy frequencies, we experience a harmonious connection with the "fount of every blessing."

The Apostle Paul referred to these higher emotions as "fruits of the spirit." He told the Galatians: "But the fruit of the Spirit is love, joy, peace, long-suffering, gentleness, goodness, faith" (Gal 5:22). Your feelings are a measure of whether you are *on-track* or *off-track* in your alignment with your Divine Purpose.

Feeling Good is feeling God

Are you happy? Being happy is one of the most important things you can do to connect with True Success! Before you begin to contemplate what you really want from life, you must start from a positive vibration. And being happy automatically puts you into the positive vibration.

So many people find it hard to identify what they want because their starting from a standpoint of stress, worry, pessimism or even doubt. When you experience these emotions, it is nearly impossible to imagine yourself out of your current situation.

Even in a neutral state you aren't aligned with True Success, because you aren't pursuing your passions. This doesn't mean being "over the top" annoyingly happy, because that cannot be maintained. There are a multitude of positive states you can be in to elicit a positive vibration. Some of these are peace, gratitude, contentment, love, appreciation, optimism, and hopefulness. All of these elicit a positive vibration. A happy positive vibration attracts the "flow" of ideas, the people, the resources and opportunities you need to succeed. Eventually you'll arrive at the point where you know that everything always works out for you. So take time to play games, do random acts of kindness, tell jokes, jump in puddles or whatever brings you happiness, and do it every day!

The Bible says that God created the world . . . and all that He created was good. Because everything that God creates is good, we can say that *good* and *God* are synonymous. When you say you want to feel good, you are really saying you want to feel God. You are saying that you want to feel the goodness that flows from God – the Source of all goodness.

We resonate with the goodness of God by feeling good. So we could say "feeling good is feeling God!"

That's why you can't get poor enough to help one person out of poverty, you can't get sick enough to help one person heal. No amount of feeling bad will connect you to your Source.

Today I challenge you to start a 10-day negativity fast. Here are the rules: If something negative happens, you have to put aside any negative emotions within 5 minutes and re-focus your attention on positive thoughts and feelings, or you have to start over at day one. You will be amazed at how inspired you will feel and the blessings you will attract into your life. If you dwell on negativity for more than 5 minutes you have to start the 10 days over again. Positive emotions connect you to the "goodness of God" and your Divine Purpose!

When you feel bad, you lose your connection to Source Energy, because you are creating resistance or *dissonance*. If your thoughts are: "I can't do this, it's not possible, I don't deserve it," you are creating resistance. You are producing emotions of fear, doubt, worry, anxiety that send out a dissonant signal.

You can use these emotions as a barometer to say to yourself: "What are the thoughts that are keeping me from the goodness of God." When you are harboring bad feelings, you're dissonant from the good that you really desire.

The Bible talks about a time when the people of Judah were facing a formidable foe, an impossible situation. God said to them "You don't have to fight this battle. Stand still and you will see the deliverance of the Lord." I have struggled in my life to just *stand still in faith*. My tendency is to try and figure everything out with my own reasoning. *Standing still* means maintaining a calm and peaceful emotional state. Your emotions are your barometer of the resonance you have with your source – the fount of every blessing. *Standing still* means feeling good so we can feel God.

Only two emotions

There are really only two major emotions, **love** and **fear**. All other emotions branch either directly or indirectly from these two. If your life is not manifesting the abundance, joy and meaning you desire, it's time to make the shift from being **"fear-based"** to being **"love-based."**

The Emotional Energy Chart below lists emotions in the order of their frequencies from highest to lowest. The emotions at the top of the chart (love, acceptance, joy, passion) are most likely to resonate with spirit. While those are the bottom (fear, despair, shame, unworthiness) are most likely to be dissonant from spirit.

By learning to maintain a high frequency, you'll become so tuned in to your spiritual source that your life becomes a joyful experience! Things you want will begin to manifest, your problems will dissipate more easily and you will begin to experience a state known as "flow."

Emotional Energy Chart
High-Frequency Emotions / Divine Purpose Emotions

1. Love / Acceptance / Joy
2. Passion
3. Enthusiasm / Eagerness / Optimism
4. Positive Expectation / Belief and Faith
5. Optimism
6. Hopefulness
7. Contentment

Low-frequency emotions

1. Boredom
2. Pessimism
3. Frustration/ Irritation / Impatience
4. Disappointment
5. Doubt
6. Worry
7. Blame
8. Discouragement
9. Anger
10. Revenge
11. Hatred

12. Jealousy

13. Shame / Guilt / Unworthiness

14. Fear / Grief / Depression / Despair / Powerlessness

What are your prevalent emotions? Gauge your connection to Divine Purpose by the emotions you are experiencing. Are your emotions resonating with Source Energy or are they limiting you to a life of dissonance? Because emotions are the result of beliefs, you must ask yourself: "What are my beliefs? Do my current beliefs limit me from receiving all of the goodness God has in store for my life?

- If you fear failure, what are the beliefs that trigger this emotion?

- If you experience feelings of shame, what are the beliefs behind it?

Love resonates with Divine Purpose

Love is a powerful spiritual emotion that vibrates at such a high frequency it resonates directly with the Source Energy.

All high frequency (spiritual) emotions such as joy, peace, inspiration . . . are merely appendages to the greatest of all emotions - love.

Fear is dissonant from Divine Purpose

The emotion of fear is at the opposite end of the spectrum. It is a low-frequency emotion.

Fearful thoughts will bring about negative emotions such as anxiety and worry. These types of emotions are often referred to as "bad vibes," and that is absolutely true. Negative emotions send out negative vibrations, and those vibrations align with and attract more of the same..

Fears that keep us from Divine Purpose can be manifested in different ways.

Fear of asking

A key component of aligning with our Divine Purpose is asking. Whether it be asking God or the Universe or other people, asking is an essential first step. In Jack Canfield's best-selling book, The Success Principles, one of the principles he emphasizes is Ask, Ask, Ask. Unfortunately, the fear of rejection keeps people from asking for and receiving that which aligns them with True Success.

Fear is projecting into the future and imagining a negative result - also known as worrying. There are two ways you can deal with this:

- Stop projecting into the future and just take action
- Project into the future, but replace the negative image with a positive image.

The main way to get past fear is simply to act, because the greatest growth is where the greatest fear is! Someone once said, "The way out is through."

Take 100% responsibility for the fact that your thoughts and emotions are creating your current reality. Don't put blame on anyone or anything. Accept the fact that you have to change your beliefs, thoughts and emotions.

Fear of Believing

Any time you experience fear of failure, what you are really experiencing is the fear of believing. It is a fear of having your belief shattered by setting your heart on something that might not happen.

When you align with your Divine Purpose, fear of failure dissipates because your belief is bolstered by the resonance you feel.

Fear of failure is a signal that we are not connecting to our divine source. It is a signal of our need to reframe our current beliefs.

All truly successful people fail their way to success. Here we must re-define what most people mean by the word failure. When Thomas Edison was asked how he felt by failing over 1000 times to get the light bulb to work he said: "I didn't fail, I found 1000 ways that it wouldn't work."

So-called failure is nothing more than feedback on how something doesn't work so that the necessary adjustments can be made. The "common denominator" in the belief systems of successful people is that they **never see failure as failure, only as the feedback necessary to make adjustments.**

Your ability to believe in your Divine Purpose, even in the face of roadblocks, will allow you to receive the feedback to overcome obstacles.

Fear of receiving

"Ever tried. Ever failed. No matter. Try again.
Fail again. Fail better"
– Samuel Beckett

As you begin receiving help from your divine source it will come in the form of "feedback." Realize that the fear of feedback is your ego, and allow all feedback as a divine gift.

"You won't believe what you can accomplish by attempting the impossible with the courage to repeatedly fail better."[20]

The following is a list of people were endowed with innate God-given gifts and talents. These are all people who were true to their Divine callings in life and although they experienced, so called, failures along the way, their true success eventually emerged.

Henry Ford: Ford is famous today for his creation of the assembly line and American-made cars, but his success didn't come quickly. In his early years his failures left him broke five times before he founded the successful Ford Motor Company.

Soichiro Honda: Honda began with a series of failures. Honda interviewed for a job with the Toyota motor company, as an engineer, but was turned down, leaving him jobless for quite some time. He started making scooters of his own at home, and finally started his own business.

Bill Gates: Gates dropped out of Harvard and started a failed first business with Microsoft co-founder Paul Allen called Traf-O-Data. His early idea didn't work, but his later work did. He created the global empire that is Microsoft.

Walt Disney:.Disney was fired by a newspaper editor because they said: "he lacked imagination and had no good ideas." Disney went on to start a number of businesses that didn't last too long and ended with bankruptcy and failure. But as he followed his passion, he eventually found a recipe for success that worked.

Albert Einstein: Einstein did not speak until he was four and did not read until he was seven, causing his teachers and parents to think he was mentally handicapped. He was expelled from school and was refused admittance to the Zurich Polytechnic School. It might have taken him a bit longer, but most people would agree that he caught on pretty well in the end, winning the Nobel Prize and changing the face of modern physics.

Isaac Newton: Newton was a genius when it came to math, but he had some failings early on. He never did particularly well in school and when put in charge of running the family farm, he failed miserably, so poorly in fact that an uncle took charge and sent him off to Cambridge where he finally blossomed into the scholar we know today.

Thomas Edison: As a child, Edison was told he was "too stupid to learn anything." He was fired from his first two jobs for not being productive enough. Even as an inventor, Edison made 1,000 unsuccessful attempts at inventing the light bulb. All of those unsuccessful attempts were necessary in helping him discover the design that worked.

Orville and Wilbur Wright: Both Orville and Wilbur struggled with depression. They eventually started a bicycle shop and that lead them to experiment with flight. After numerous attempts, and tons of failed prototypes, they finally created a plane that could get airborne and stay there.

Winston Churchill: Churchill failed the sixth grade. Later in life he faced many years of political failures. He was defeated in every election for public office until he finally became the Prime Minister at the age of 62.

Abraham Lincoln: In his youth he went to war a captain and returned a private (if you're not familiar with military ranks, just know that private is as low as it goes.) Lincoln didn't stop failing there, however. He started numerous failed businesses and was defeated in numerous runs he made for public office.

Jerry Seinfeld: The first time the Jerry walked on stage at a comedy club, he looked out at the audience, froze and was eventually jeered and booed off of the stage. Seinfeld believed he could do it, so he went back the next night, completed his set to laughter and applause, and the rest is history.

Harrison Ford: Ford was told by the movie execs that he simply didn't have what it takes to be a star. Today, Ford can proudly show that he does, in fact, have what it takes.

Steven Spielberg: Spielberg was rejected from the University of Southern California School of Theater, Film and Television three times. He eventually tried another school, only to drop out to become a director before finishing. Thirty-five years after starting his degree, Spielberg returned to school in 2002 to finally complete his work and earn his BA.

J. K. Rowling: Rowling was nearly penniless, severely depressed, divorced, trying to raise a child on her own while attending school and writing a novel. Rowling went from depending on welfare to survive to being one of the richest women in the world in a span of only five years by being true to what resonated for her. This gave her the energy and determination to persit.

Jack London: London published popular novels like White Fang and The Call of the Wild, his first story received six hundred rejection slips before finally being accepted.

Michael Jordan: Jordan was actually cut from his high school basketball team. Luckily, Jordan didn't let this setback stop him from playing the game he loved. Jordan later said: "I have missed more than 9,000 shots in my career. I have lost almost 300 games. On 26 occasions I have been entrusted to take the game winning shot, and I missed. I have failed over and over and over again in my life. And that is why I succeed."

Babe Ruth: Ruth held the record for strikeouts for decades. His attitude was simply this:, "Every strike brings me closer to the next home run."

Just like each of these people on my list, your contribution to the world is vitally important. You have innate skills and abilities that need to be shared. An important belief of truly successful people is the belief that the events of their lives happen for a reason – they happen for their good! Jack Canfield teaches of a process he terms being a "reverse paranoid." Rather than believing the "world is out to get you," you believe that it's working for your good.

"We know that all things work together for good to them that love God" (Romans 8:28) – The Apostle Paul

Create new beliefs that make you feel grateful. Gratitude is one of the most powerful emotions in connecting you to divine purpose, and it just feels good. If you believe that everything is happening for your good, you are always looking for the good in life. You will be constantly "tuned in" to the positive energy in your life.

Words are Energy

"With your words, you set into motion the direction your life will go. That's why it is so important for us to get in agreement with God and speak the goodness, favor and blessing of God over our lives."

— Joel Osteen

Just avoiding negative talk is not enough, you must go on the offensive! Don't use words to describe your current situation; use your words to change it!

When you speak words of faith and promise into your life, you are actually calling out the potential God has placed inside you.

Words ignite the greatness in you.

So many times, people focus on the negative things in life. They don't realize that they have incredible gifts, potential and talents lying dormant, just waiting to be called into action. Speaking negative words is like dropping an anchor right where you are.

But when you begin to declare the blessings and favor of Almighty God, you're pulling up that anchor and hoisting your sails. You're positioning yourself to catch the winds of God's favor.

Today it's time to declare, "I am a strong, equipped, empowered, anointed child of the Most High God. I'm not second-class. I'm not ordinary. I've been handpicked by the Creator of the universe. I have great things in my future!"

When you speak life-changing words, the winds begin to shift in your direction. God fills those sails of faith and sets you on a greater course than you could have ever imagined.

Sometimes, it only takes one word — one encouragement — to

ignite the greatness on the inside of you." (Email I received about his CD's, the Power of Your Words)

Summary
How do I apply this principle?

- Paying attention to your vibrational signal
- Recognizing what thoughts and emotions determine that signal
- Recognizing where your emotions fall on the emotion chart

Benefits

- Gaining an awareness of how you are responsible for what is manifesting in your life.
- Gaining an awareness of emotions that resonate with Source energy.

Consequences

- Remaining dissonant from Source energy
- Being shut off from the "flow" of True Success

CHAPTER 3

How to Reprogram your Conscious Mind to Raise your Frequency!
Principle #3: Choose Your Focus

> *"Its God's job to provide 'the way,' it's our job to choose our focus."*

While I was learning these principles I was going through a very difficult time financially, spiritually and emotionally. What I saw in my current reality was discouraging, and I had formed the habit of focusing on how bad things were.

I had to make a choice of either continuing to focus on the problems and challenges that were all around me or begin choosing to focus on things that inspire me, bring me joy, make me feel grateful, and connect me with True Success.

This caused me to come face to face with the fact that I am 100% responsible for my own beliefs, thoughts and emotions, as well as, the energy they transmit. I found that focusing on those things that brought me joy, actually connected me to the meaningful and purposeful life I desired.

As I started practicing these principles it seemed that things were beginning to fall apart. Wasn't I supposed to be attracting success and abundance? As you start practicing a connection to joy, passion and gratitude, old things will fall out of your life, and it can be easy to see that as failure.

At first I believed that the principles weren't working, but once I "let go" and allowed the flow of Divine help, it seemed like miracles began to happen .   As I began writing this book I had the opportunity to be interviewed by Jack Canfield to a world-wide audience. This interview just came to me without having to seek it out. Another opportunity that came to me without seeking it was being featured on the Wall Street Journal Live TV show and being interview for an article in the Wall Street Journal.

I suddenly found myself with opportunities to connect with some of the top authors, speakers and coaches in my niche; people like Ann McIndoo, Steve Harrison, Bob Doyle and Christy Whitman. I was being inspired about the next steps to take and being led to mentors and coaches that helped me take the next steps.

The conscious mind is reprogramed through using the principle of agency to choose our focus. With an understanding of the principles of resonance and universal energy, I was ready to choose a focus that was purposeful. The principle of agency enables us to believe, think and feel in ways that transmit a higher vibrational signal.

Choose your focus

"Where your focus goes, energy flows."
Tony Robbins

Most people focus on "how it is." For example: I am in debt. I am overweight. I am alone. The world is a mess. But great power comes from focusing on "what can be"as if it already is: I am debt-free. I maintain a healthy weight. I am supported by other people. I am making a difference in the world.

In life you will have problems, but you have the ability to choose your focus. You can choose to focus on the "goodness of God," and believe that a Higher Power is greater than your problems. You must make the choice to keep your mind focused on things that will create a high vibrational signal.

Some people say "when my situation turns around then I'll cheer up," but it doesn't work that way. You must cheer up first. You must create a vibrational connection with the goodness of God and then your situation will turn around. As long as you harbor a poor, defeated outlook you will remain in a dissonant, defeated life.

Whatever you focus on will manifest in a greater degree. That is why you cannot focus on your problems. You cannot focus on what is missing. You cannot focus on your weaknesses or where you fall short. Choose to focus on your strengths instead of your weaknesses. People are usually gifted in one or two areas and mediocre in the all the rest. We can choose to focus on mastery in the areas we are gifted at, or we can struggle to become average in all the rest.

Focusing on these types of things will weaken your energy signal:

- Complaining
- Worrying
- Obsessing/fretting
- Wishing things were different
- Fighting/arguing
- Regretting past actions/decisions

Choose instead to focus on:

- Things that are going right for you.
- Things you are looking forward to.
- Things that make you feel good.
- Things you really enjoy.
- Things you really appreciate.
- Memories that make you laugh or feel good.
- People who love you and people you love.
- Anything positive you see in your daily life, like a baby laughing, beautiful clouds in the sky, or how delicious your lunch is.

As you choose a higher focus, you'll see more examples of generosity, kindness, humor, love, joy, and gratitude that make you think, "Oh, there's something else positive I can focus on . . ."

Then come the positive feelings – you'll notice that you feel lighter, happier, less weighed down by problems, even if every problem doesn't vanish instantly. They just won't have such a strong impact on you.

Neuroplasticity

The word "plasticity" comes from the Greek word plastikos, meaning "formed" or "molded." As you might guess, "neuroplasticity" refers the now common idea that we are not born with brains that are fixed. They continue to change throughout our lives. Our neural pathways get set up by habitual ways of thinking and just like we can correct a bad golf swing, we can also correct bad thinking patterns. Neural Scientists have found that people who meditate can change the neural activity in their brains and actually change the size of certain parts of the brain..

"Neuroplasticity is a process that results in a change of the brains structure, circuits, chemical composition, or functions. It is best understood as a capacity (or potential) for brain areas and circuits to take on new roles or functions."[21]

"On its own, neuroplasticity is neither good nor bad. It is simply a brain mechanism that developed to help us adapt to our environment and survive changing conditions. The real power is in the concept of Self-directed Neuroplasticity, because it gives you a say in what happens to you and how your brain is wired."[22]

Self-Directed Neuroplasticity is using **the power of focused attention**, along with the ability to apply commitment, hard work, and dedication, to direct your choices and actions, thereby re-wiring your brain to work for you and with your true self."

In other words, we shape the circuitry of our brains by what we continuously choose to focus on, even though we may do this subconsciously. This is how our dominant thoughts create our reality.

The point to remember is that neuroplasticity is happening all the time. We are constantly affecting the chemistry of our brains by the things we choose to focus on.

This is why choosing to align with Divine Purpose is so important. As you choose to focus your beliefs, thoughts and emotions in ways that resonate with Divine Intelligence, new neural pathways assist you in connecting to Divine Purpose! . Jack Canfield referred to it as our "Divine Obsession." In other words, focusing on Divine Purpose leads to chemical changes in the brain that align with who you are intended to be.

Does your current mindset enable you to see and believe in limitless possibilities or does it keep you locked into seeing limitations? The principle of agency will help you gain a mindset of faith and expectancy so you can enter your promised land of Divine Purpose!

Choose to build your cathedral!

Even though everyone told him it couldn't be done, Pablo Coelho had a dream of being a writer. His father told him, "Get a job as an engineer like me and then you can write in your spare time." Pablo's response was, "This does not work! You have to know the meaning of your life!"

Your Divine purpose is not something you do in your spare time! You have to choose to be totally committed! This way you cannot fail because your life will have meaning and you will create joy every single day.

Pablo tells a wonderful story about three men who were working on a building. When a curious person passed by, he asked the first builder, "What are you doing?" The builder said, "Can't you see? I'm cutting stones."

Unsatisfied with the first man's answer, he moved to the second person and asked, "What are you doing here?" And the second person said, "Can't you see? I'm earning my living. I have a family to provide for." The passerby realized that at least the second person had a purpose. He was doing his work for the love of his family.

Then the passerby went to the third person and asked, "What are you doing here?" And the third person answered, "Can't you see? I'm building a cathedral." The third person saw his Divine Purpose.

The first man's focus was on his physical work. The second man's focus was on a purpose, but the third man resonated with his Divine Purpose.[23]

Don't spend your life working for survival! Choose to build your cathedral. Your cathedral is what you give to life, because life is very generous to you!

Your ability to resonate with Divine Purpose depends upon the choices you are willing to make. Your ability to make those choices is often shaped in the "refiner's fire" of your life's adversities. Your greatest learning experiences rarely come when you are sitting at the top of the mountain of success. You are most likely sitting at the top of the mountain as a result of your choices made in the "refiner's fire."

Earlier in my life, I was a success-driven sales person, loving the big bonus checks, profit sharing, stock options and incentive trips to London, Hawaii, New York, and the Caribbean. But even with all that so- called success, something was wrong. I was stressed out and beginning to experience severe panic attacks and depression. Although my health was a problem, I continued driving myself to live the "common denominator of success" -doing the things that unsuccessful people weren't willing to do.

Eventually the stress and anxiety began to take their toll and I could no longer maintain the level of sales success I was accustomed to.

I left the company after 24 years, believing I needed a new start. What followed was the greatest test of my life. I experienced a number of failures as I tried to start a new career, but the eventual result was financial failure, debt, and the loss of my life savings.

Not only did I suffer a financial collapse, but I also suffered a loss of confidence and purpose.

As the economy got worse, I feared the possible loss of my low-paying salaried job. I decided to start my own business and began pushing myself so hard to get the business off the ground that I suffered a heart attack at the age of 49.

As I continued trying to build my business , I found myself taking menial jobs in order to just keep things afloat. I found myself at "rock bottom" asking myself, "How did I get here?" Many of my old friends from my sales career were still winning their incentive trips and getting their big bonus checks. Some were now retiring on the profit sharing and stock options that I had lost.

My wife had seen a PBS special where Wayne Dyer talked about the "the spirit of intention" and she decided "enough was enough.," We were going to begin learning and applying Universal laws. We were going to start putting our beliefs, thoughts and emotions in alignment with the source of all goodness.

What I hadn't realized was that during this difficult time in my life, universal principles were already at work manifesting energy that was a vibrational match for my negative emotions. Universal principles don't show favoritism, they just work according to universal laws.

The downward spiral I was on helped me see that I had a choice to make. I could continue on this path or I could choose to "build my cathedral." My cathedral, or Divine Purpose is doing what resonates with me more than anything else - uplifting and inspiring people through writing, speaking and coaching. My cathedral is helping people remove limiting beliefs and align with Divine Purpose!

What are the Keys of True Success?

*"Your life is the result of the choices you make
. . . If you don't like your life, it's time to start
making better choices"*
>   - Unknown

Ask, Believe and Receive

*"Our doubts are traitors, and make us lose the
good we oft might win, by fearing to attempt."*
>   – William Shakespeare

The formula for True Success is so simple that most people can't believe or accept it. The formula is simply this: Ask, Believe and Receive.

All three parts of the formula are things you must choose. You must choose to ask, you must choose to believe, and you must choose to receive.

Choose to Ask

Nothing really happens until you are willing to ask. Until you ask there is nothing to believe in and there is nothing to be received. Ask God, your higher power and others for help, for guidance, for mentoring, for knowledge, for inspiration, for solutions.

Ask, and it shall be given you; seek, and ye shall find; knock, and it shall be opened unto you. For every one that asketh receiveth; and he that seeketh findeth; and to him that knocketh it shall be opened. (Matt 7:7-8)

Choose to Believe

Dr. Norman Vincent Peale, put it this way: "This is one of the greatest laws in the universe, fervently so I wish I had discovered it as a very young man. It dawned upon me much later in life, and I have found it to be one of my greatest – if not my greatest – discovery, outside of my relationship with God . . . The great law briefly and simply stated is that if you think in negative terms, you will get negative results. If you think in positive terms, you will achieve positive results." "That is a simple fact," he went on to say, "which is the basis of an astonishing law of prosperity and success. In three words: Believe and succeed."[24]

Once upon a time, there was a large mountainside, where an eagle's nest rested. The eagle's nest contained four large eagle eggs. One day an earthquake rocked the mountain causing one of the eggs to roll down the mountain, to a chicken farm, located in the valley below. The chickens knew that they must protect and care for the eagle's egg, so an old hen volunteered to nurture and raise the large egg.

One day, the egg hatched and a beautiful eagle was born. Sadly, however, the eagle was raised to be a chicken. Soon, the eagle believed he was nothing more than a chicken. The eagle loved his home and family, but his spirit cried out for more. While playing a game on the farm one day, the eagle looked to the skies above and noticed a group of mighty eagles soaring in the skies. "Oh," the eagle cried, "I wish I could soar like those birds." The chickens roared with laughter, "You cannot soar with those birds. You are a chicken and chickens do not soar."

The eagle continued staring, at his real family up above, dreaming that he could be with them. Each time the eagle would let his dreams be known, he was told it couldn't be done. That is what the eagle learned to believe. The eagle, after time, stopped dreaming and continued to live his life like a chicken. Finally, after a long life as a chicken, the eagle passed away.

The moral of the story: You become what you believe you are; so if you ever dream to become an eagle follow your dreams, not the words of a chicken. – Source unknown

Unlike the eagle who failed to believe in his divine purpose, Abraham chose to believe God when he told him he would be the father of many nations, even though it didn't seem possible in the natural realm. Abraham knew God had a divine purpose for his life. It resonated with him spiritually even though he couldn't see it in the natural realm.

Each of us is meant "to fly!" Flying, so to speak is our Divine Purpose, but belief is the key to activating that power. The word "believe" is a verb! Verbs indicate taking action on something. It indicates choosing to set your mind firmly on something of importance to you. To believe in your Divine Purpose is to set your mind firmly upon it and to think about it every night and day!

What is your current concept of God or a Higher Power? Were you raised to believe in a judgmental, cruel God? Have you prayed for help and gotten no response so many times that you eventually stopped believing in divinity? Or have you always had a difficult time believing in any concept of God or spirit?

Even if your feelings and beliefs on this subject aren't completely clear to you, it's important to ask yourself: In general, do I see Universal Laws as friend or foe? Do I believe Universal Laws are working for me or against me?

Choose to believe that circumstances will work out in your favor. Choose to trust that Divine Intelligence iw working on your behalf.

As you start seeing results from smaller situations, you'll be more confident trusting that Universal laws are at work   helping you with larger ones too!

Keep in mind that you can't build unshakable trust in just one day. This will be a process of steadily trusting, seeing the proof, trusting a bit more, seeing more proof, until finally you realize one day that you just don't have any more doubts.

Changing your thoughts, feelings and beliefs really works if you put the effort into it, by "thinking about it every night and day."

Choose to Receive

If I had a thousand gallons of water to give you but you only had a one-gallon container, you wouldn't be able to receive what I had for you. The problem would not be with the supply. It would be with your capacity to receive. If you would get rid of the small container and get something larger, I could give you so much more.

Divine intelligence is available to you in unlimited supply. "According to your faith it will be done unto you." Source energy is unlimited and infinite resources are available to you. The supply you receive will be according to what you allow yourself to receive. .

Today, get rid of your small container, increase your capacity to believe and receive. Enlarge your thinking and connect to your Divine Purpose!

Joel Osteen in his book "Your Best Life Now" shared this great story that illustrates our need to expand our capacity to receive:

Years ago, before transatlantic flight was common, a man wanted to travel to the United States from Europe. The man worked hard, saved every extra penny he could, and finally had just enough money to purchase a ticket aboard a cruise ship. The trip at that time required about two of three weeks to cross the ocean. He went out and bought a suitcase and filled it full of cheese and crackers. That's all he could afford.

Once on board, all the other passengers went to the large, ornate dining room to eat their gourmet meals. Meanwhile, the poor man would go over in the corner and eat his cheese and crackers. This went on day after day. He could smell the delicious food being served in the dining room. He heard the other passengers speak of it in glowing terms as they rubbed their bellies and complained of how full they were, and how they would have to go on a diet after this trip. The poor traveler wanted to join the other guests in the dining room, but he had no extra money. Sometimes he'd lie awake at night, dreaming of the sumptuous meals the other guests described.

Toward the end of the trip, another man came up to him and said, "Sir, I can't help but notice that you are always over there eating those cheese and crackers at mealtimes. Why don't you come into the banquet hall and eat with us?

The traveler's face flushed with embarrassment. "Well, to tell you the truth, I had only enough money to buy the ticket. I don't have any extra money to purchase the fancy meals."

The other passenger raised his eyebrows in surprise. He shook his head and said, "Sir, don't you realize the meals are included in the price of the ticket? Your meals have already been paid for!"

When you go through life living in a state of separation from your divine purpose, you are choosing to eat cheese and crackers rather than coming into the feast that has already been prepared for you. Your divine purpose is a fabulous banquet complete with every good thing imaginable and it has already been paid for.

Divine Intelligence is a field of infinite energy. Your Divine Purpose is connected to a powerful source of abundance that you have access to. Abundance is strongly linked to your Divine Purpose for one major reason: when you are focused on something that's really important to you, something you really love, something that allows you to use your skills and talents in a positive way, it boosts your vibrational frequency!

Did you know that this Divine Intelligence has already released good things into your future? It covers your entire lifetime! It includesthe right people, the right circumstances, and the right breaks. Today, no matter what you may be facing, focus on moving forward. Divine intelligence will order your steps and arranged good things for you. Maybe you've heard the phrase, "Do what you love and the money will follow"? When you spend time doing something that you truly enjoy, you quickly come into alignment with the essence of abundance, which means you become receptive to all kinds of great opportunities and of course, more money. That doesn't necessarily mean that your purpose has to be your career, however. It's very possible to have a purpose that doesn't directly bring money into your life.

In fact, this is a big stumbling block for a lot of people who know what they'd like to be doing for their purpose, but they can't see any way to receive enough money from doing it. If you have the same concerns, let them go. Instead, intend that you can allow as much money as you want into your life, no matter how it comes to you, and even if it doesn't come in ways you expected.

Key #1 - Choose Beliefs that Align with Divine Purpose

> *"We are the masters of our earthly destinies in that we have the power to influence our own subconscious mind, and through it gain the cooperation of infinite intelligence."*
>
> – Napoleon Hill

We all have the means to connect to Divine Purpose, but we often keep ourselves from it by holding onto dissonant beliefs, thoughts and emotions.

We have a Divine Purpose! And with the principle of agency and other Universal principles, we can access everything for its fulfillment.

> *"You have many choices. You can choose forgiveness over revenge, joy over despair. You can choose action over apathy."*
>
> - Stephanie Marston

We must choose each day to maintain our connection with our Higher Power. And times of adversity require that we choose faith. Although each of us has a Divine Purpose, it is never forced upon us. We must rise to it, and connect with it, through the use of our agency. The gifts, talents, passions and dreams that we have inherited are intended for our Divine Purpose, but we must choose to align with them.

How do we choose our Divine Purpose? We choose it by following our dreams and passions.

The gift of agency makes you responsible for your choices. In fact it makes you responsible for everything that manifests in your life. You have the power to choose beliefs, thoughts and emotions that resonate with your Divine Purpose, or choosing those that keep you dissonant. You choose Divine Purpose by choosing to resonate with it.

Story of Stanley Praimnath

Stanley's life has undergone some major changes in the last 10 years.. Those major changes have caused him to think of what Joseph said to his brothers, "You meant evil against me but God meant it for good."

Even before the events of September 11, he was troubled by a nightmare. In the dream Stanley said that he could hear someone speaking to him, but he had no idea who it was, but the voice kept saying, "You're not doing what you're supposed to do, Stanley."

Stanley was an investment banker who miraculously survived an escape from the 81st floor of the World Trade Center partly due to the help of a man he'd never met named Brian Clark, who stopped to help him on his way down from his office three floors above.

Later, Stanley went around the country speaking to church groups, telling his story: "I was in Springfield, Missouri, when I had the nightmare again. I met with a pastor the next day and he noticed that I was upset. I told him about my nightmares.

"May I pray for you?" he asked.

"Absolutely," I said.

He laid his hands on my head and prayed. In that moment it was like someone flipped a light on in my soul. I suddenly knew what I had to do.

I enrolled in Global University, an online Bible college. I read the Bible and my course books when I got home from work, studying every night from 9:30 p.m. to 2 a.m. A year later, I finished the program. I'm now a fully certified minister."

Stanley still works as an investment banker for a different bank. It grew too difficult for him to go back to the office with so many friends gone. The very first day he sent out his résumé, he got a call from a man he'd worked with a decade earlier, who now was a director for Royal Bank of Scotland. 'I thought you died,' he said.

"No," he told him. "I lived. Thank the Lord. I lived." Stanley got the job.

Stanley and his wife, Jennifer hardly talk about what happened. Lot's wife looked back; Stanley believes in looking forward. There's a lot to look forward to these days, a lot to be grateful for. His daughter Stephanie is 18 now, and is going to St. Francis College. She hopes to become a school teacher one day. His little one, Caitlin, is 14 and starting high school this year. He says his family has grown much closer since 9/11. He knows now to spend less time at work and more time enjoying his family.

He and Brian are brothers for life. This year, on September 11, they'll get together at his church in Ozone Park, New York, and tell the congregation about what God did for them 10 years ago. Stanley plans to bring the shoes he wore to work that day. The soles are melted and they're caked in ash. He keeps them in a shoebox with the word "deliverance" written all around it. They're kind of like his ark, a reminder of God's presence and the life he owe to him.

Stanley chooses to believe in looking forward. He chooses to believe that God meant his experience to be for his good. He chose to believe that his life was spared for a Divine Purpose yet to be completed. Although Stanley's experience didn't change his main occupation, it helped him see and believe in a deeper purpose - a ministry right where he was.[25]

No matter what "chains" you may feel like you are in today, remember, your Divine Source can fill you with power.

When doors look closed all around you, when your surroundings look limited, when you feel like you're in chains, remember, Universal Laws are always at work. Keep your hopes up. Keep expecting. Keep believing.

None of us are victims to our circumstances. None of us are consigned to an empty and meaningless life. Each of us has the gift and power of agency. We have the power to choose what we will believe, think and feel.

> *"If thou canst believe, all things are possible to him that believeth."*
>
> (Mark9:23)

Choose to be true to your purpose

I recently learned about a nurse whose job is to take care of people who are close to death. She asked hundreds of her patients in the last weeks of their lives what their biggest regret was. The number one regret reported was, "I wish I had been true to who I was and not just lived to meet the expectations of others."

How many people today are not being true to who they were created to be simply because they are afraid of disappointing someone? They have a desperate need to be accepted into a certain group. You cannot live trying to be who your parents want you to be, or who your boss wants you to be, or who your friends want you to be. You've got to stay true to to living your divine purpose!

Hold your attention on your intended outcome with unbending purpose! Absolutely refuse to allow obstacles to dissipate the focused quality of your attention! Do this to the exclusion of all obstacles and you will be able to maintain unshakable serenity and be committed to your goal with intense passion.

Surrender yourself wholeheartedly to your dreams and passions. They are there to direct you to your divine purpose. Let it mold and shape your character. Let it order your steps. As you submit to a life of divine purpose, you will live the fulfilled, abundant life that has been prepared for you!

Choose to find meaning

> *"Everyone has his own specific vocation or mission in life Therein he cannot be replaced, nor can his life be repeated. Thus, everyones task is as unique as is his specific opportunity to implement it.*
>
> -Viktor Frankl

My daughter, who can be quite blunt, recently sent me an email that said: "Everything happens for a reason, but sometimes that reason is that you are stupid and you make bad decisions." I don't know how helpful that statement was for my belief system, but it was a reminder that I do have the power to choose how I will interpret the meaning of my life's events. The meaning that we assign to our life's events will either empower us or weaken us, so we must choose carefully.

The people who inspire me the most are not people with lives of ease, but the people who have had the most to overcome. All problems contain seeds of opportunity. Every upsetting situation can become an opportunity for the creation of something new and beautiful. Often it is in our times of greatest trial that we find the need for our Divine Purpose. Refining fires give us a deeper compassion for others who are going through similar trials. These experiences become part of our story that can be a great inspiration to others. They are part of a divine design, giving us the compassion and vision to fulfill our ultimate calling. When you pray for a miracle that does not come to pass, maybe it's because you are intended to be the miracle for someone else. Your Divine Purpose may well be the miracle that other people are praying for.

The years of 1942 to 1945 were an indescribable nightmare for a man named Victor Frankl. He endured the horror of the Nazi death camps. It was only through his willingness to choose the meaning of his trials that he was able to survive the hellish experiences and know his Divine Purpose.

Victor chose to believe that we cannot avoid suffering but we can find meaning in it and move forward with renewed purpose. He insisted that our primary drive in life is not pleasure; it is the discovery and pursuit of meaning.

He said: "We who lived in the concentration camps can remember the men who walked through the huts comforting others, giving away their last piece of bread. They may have been few in number, but they offer sufficient proof that everything can be taken from a man but one thing: the last of the human freedoms - to choose one's attitude in any given set of circumstances, to choose one's way."

I love Viktor Frankl's quote: "When we are no longer able to change a situation, we are challenged to change ourselves."

And there were always choices to make. Every day, every hour he was offered the opportunity to make a decision, he described it as "a decision whether you would or would not submit to those powers which threatened to rob you of your very self, your inner freedom; which determined whether or not you would become the plaything of circumstance, renouncing freedom and dignity to become molded into the form of a typical inmate."[26]

Nick Vujicic, was born in 1982 in Melbourne, Australia. without arms nor legs. A limbless son was not what his parents had been expecting. His mother was a nurse and his father was a Pastor..Like any parents would, they asked themselves questions, like: How would their son live a normal happy life? What could he ever do or become when living with such a massive disability? Little did they or anyone else know that this beautiful limbless baby would one day be someone who would inspire and motivate people from all walks of life. Nick came to realize his Divine Purpose and he is living his passion as he inspires people all around the world.

Although Nick found his purpose in life, he was not immune to the typical challenges of school and adolescence such as bullying and self-esteem issues. Nick struggled with depression and loneliness. He constantly questioned why he was different than all the other kids surrounding him; why he was the one born without arms and legs. He wondered what the purpose behind his life was, or if he even had a purpose. According to Nick, the victory over his struggles throughout his journey, as well as the strength and passion he has for life can be credited to his faith in God. His family, friends and the many people he has encountered along the way have also encouraged him.

After school, Nick went on with further study and obtained a double Bachelor's degree, majoring in Accounting and Financial Planning from Griffith University in Logan, Australia. By the age of 19, Nick started to realize his innate gift of being able to inspire and encourage people by sharing his testimony about how God changed his life and gave him a future and a hope. "I found the purpose of my existence, and also the purpose of my circumstance. There's a purpose for why you're in the fire." Nick wholeheartedly believes that there is a purpose in the struggles we each encounter in our lives, and that our attitude towards those struggles, along with our faith and trust in the Lord can be the keys to overcoming the challenges we face.

Today, this limbless young man has accomplished more than most people accomplish in a lifetime. Nick made the massive move from Brisbane, Australia to California, USA in 2007, where he is the President and CEO of a non-profit organization, Life Without Limbs. Since his first speaking engagement back when he was 19, Nick has traveled around the world, sharing his story with millions of people, speaking to a range of different groups such as students, teachers, youth, businessmen and women, entrepreneurs, and church congregations of all sizes. He has also told his story and been interviewed on various televised programs worldwide. "If God can use a man without arms and legs to be His hands and feet, then He will certainly use any willing heart!"[27]

Even though Nick could have chosen to believe that his life held no meaning or purpose because of his disabilities, he chose instead to give it meaning by inspiring millions of people

Our Divine Purpose, endows each of us with the right to choose meaning in everything that happens to us. We can choose to believe that everything happens for a reason, and it serves us. We can choose to believe that all things are working for our good."

Choose your Paradigms

"Sometimes in tragedy we find our life's purpose"
– Robert Brault

There are two things we must be aware of in order to create True Success. First, we must be aware of where we are, and second, we must place our focus on where we're going, then we must keep moving in the direction of our focus.

The real problem that keeps people from True Success is the first part: where you are. The paradigm of where you are is what is keeping you stuck mentally.

Our paradigms can cause huge challenges in our lives. They cost us purpose and passion, as well as time and money. The problem with paradigms is that they shape our logic. It wasn't that long ago when people believed the world was flat, and that was logical, in fact to think otherwise was heresy.

It was a very short time ago, just 100 years , that it was believed that anything heavier than air could not fly. The Wright Brothers went to the other side of logic when they challenged this paradigm. How about Thomas Edison's idea? People must have thought he was crazy when he said he was going to make a light. And if someone would have told me when I was a little boy what my kids are doing today with smart phones, I would have thought they were crazy.

Never allow your current paradigms to keep you from aligning with True Success., If you can visualize it in your mind, it can manifest in your life.

I encourage you to examine your current paradigms and ask yourself, "Is this empowering me or disempowering me? Is it opening my mind to endless opportunities, or is it causing me to only see dead ends? Is my current paradigm inspiring me to look at my dreams and passions, and like the Wright Brother, say 'what lies on the other side of logic?' Is it making my life exciting and filling me with passion and purpose?" If you are not able to look at your life from the perspective of "what's possible?" then re-examine your paradigms!

Choose to Dream

"Never give up on a dream just because of the time it will take to accomplish it. The time will pass anyway."

- Unknown

Maybe at one time you had a dream, but you went through some disappointments or setbacks. Things didn't turn out the way you planned. But here's a key: when one dream dies, choose to dream another dream. Just because it didn't work out the way you had it planned doesn't mean that their isn't another plan. You cannot allow one disappointment or even a series of disappointments to convince you that your dream is over. It's time to dig your heals in and hold on to the promises in your heart. Your dreams aren't random desires they are the method by which your Divine Purpose communicates with your subconscious. Your dreams enable you to fulfill your Divine Purpose. If you are dreaming of something it's because you're meant to do it.

The world needs you to fulfill your unique purpose by bringing your dreams to life. Millions of people you'll never meet will benefit whenever you take action on your dreams -particularly when your dreams are in the service of your highest good and those of humanity.

"I don't dream at night, I dream all day. I dream for a living."

– Steven Spielberg

In the musical "South Pacific" they sing a song that says "If you don't have a dream, how you gonna have a dream come true?" It doesn't take any more time to dream a big dream than it does to dream a small dream. So if you're going to dream, why not dream as big as you want? Walt Disney said, "If you can dream it you can do it!"

You wouldn't have the dream inside you if you didn't have the capacity to actually fulfill that dream. It wouldn't even occur to you to even think it.

"You're never given a dream unless you're given the ability to make that dream come true." –Richard Bach

Now is a good time to stop and begin writing down a list of your dreams. Stop now and do it!

When I wrote my first book, I had no idea how many lives would be affected by it. I received emails from people I knew back in high school, who are now living far away, that had somehow connected with my book and been deeply touched by it. I've received reports of people in other countries from Spain to South Africa whose lives were touched by it as well.

Your dreams always resonate with your higher purpose. If you follow your dreams, your dreams will manifest in your life.

Each dream - no matter how big or small - plays an important role in helping you be the person you were meant to be, and live the life we're meant to live. Don't let your dreams die inside you!

Don't be afraid to dream big dreams! Tim Ferriss in his book "The 4-Hour Work Week" said: "Having an unusually large goal is an adrenaline infusion that provides the endurance to overcome the inevitable trials and tribulations that go along with any goal. Realistic goals, goals restricted to the average ambition level, are uninspiring and will only fuel you through the first or second problem, at which point you throw in the towel. If the potential payoff is mediocre or average, so is your effort."[28] A dream worth dreaming is a dream worth going to battle for!

Just because you have a Higher Purpose doesn't mean it's going to come to pass without any opposition. Our Divine Purpose will mature us and prepare us to handle the challenges that lie in store.

You may have a dream in your heart that seems a million miles away, but Divine Purpose will take you from the prison to the palace.. During the growing process, stay focused on your dreams and passion and allow them to emerge in your life. In June of 1940, a premature baby girl was born to a poor African-American family in St. Bethlehem, TN. Wilma Rudolph, who weighed less than 5 lbs. when she was born, was one of 22 children. She was a sickly child, and when she was four, polio robbed her of the use of her left leg. The doctors put a metal brace on her leg and said she would never walk again. Day after day, she watched her brothers and sisters running and playing, but she couldn't join in.

Wilma's father worked as a railway porter, and her mother cleaned houses six days a week. They couldn't give their crippled daughter luxuries, but the simple gifts they gave – a strong work ethic and a can-do attitude – helped her through many hard times. Since her parents were unable to afford professional treatment, her mother, Blanche, learned to do massage therapy with her daughter at home.

After five years of home therapy, Wilma stunned her family and her doctors by removing the brace and walking on her own. After all those years, she could play with her brothers and sisters. She later told the Chicago Tribune, "By the time I was 12, I was challenging every boy in our neighborhood at running, jumping, everything."

As a freshman in high school, Wilma worked hard to convince the basketball coach to let her tryout. Reluctantly, he put her on the team but then cut her the same year. She was finally given a place on the team only because her father insisted that if the coach wanted Wilma's older sister to play, he would have to take Wilma too. That coach must have been amazed when, during her sophomore year, Wilma scored 803 points in 25 games setting a new state record.

To keep busy between basketball seasons, Wilma started running. At the age of 16, she qualified for the Olympics in Melbourne, Australia – although she had never even heard of the Olympics before high school. She came home with a bronze medal. Not bad for a girl who started life in a leg brace – but there was more to come.

In 1957, she enrolled at Tennessee State, where she took courses in Elementary Education and played for the women's basketball team, the Tigerbells. In her spare time, she started training as a runner. Exhausted by this new schedule, she was too sick to run for most of 1958. The next year she pulled a muscle during a crucial meet and faced another time-out of recovery.

She could easily have given up at this point. After all, she had come so far and had a bronze medal to prove it, but she didn't want to settle for third place. Somehow she found the strength to work through recovery in time to qualify for the 1960 Olympics in Rome.

In the 100 meter dash and 200 meter dash, Wilma finished at least three yards in front of her closest competitors. Then she brought her 400-meter relay team from behind to a surprise victory. She became the first woman to win three gold medals in track and field in the Olympic games. In the 1960's, she was considered the fastest woman in the world and was named the Associated Press Woman Athlete Year twice. She was honored with parades and an invitation to the White House from President John F. Kennedy. In 1983, Rudolph was inducted into the Olympic Hall of Fame. Each year the Woman's Sports Foundation presents the Wilma Rudolph Courage Award to a woman athlete who overcomes adversity, makes a significant contribution to athletics, and serves as a role model for all who face and triumph over challenges.

How did Wilma Rudolph overcome her childhood illness and poverty to make her dreams come true?. "My doctors told me I would never walk again," said Wilma. "My mother told me I would. I believed my mother." Wilma's story demonstrates how holding on and believeing in your dream can change the course of your life! Believing in a dream can take you from seemingly insurmountable adversity to stunning achievement.

> *"All our dreams can come true – if we have the courage to pursue them."*
>
> – Walt Disney

Key #2 - Choose Thoughts that Align with Divine Purpose

> *"Worrying does not empty tomorrow of its troubles, it empties today of its strength."*
>
> -Unknown

"Here's the key to success and the key to failure: "We become what we think about . . . Throughout all history, the great wise men and teachers, philosophers, and prophets have disagreed with one another on many different things. It is only on this one point that they are in complete agreement.

Consider what Marcus Aurelius, the great Roman Emperor, said: "A man's life is what his thoughts make of it." Benjamin Disraeli said this: "Everything comes if a man will only wait. I have brought myself by long meditation to the conviction that a human being with a settled purpose must accomplish it, and that nothing can resist a will that will stake even existence for its fulfillment.[29]" Ralph Waldo Emerson said this: "A man is what he thinks about all day long."

William James said: "The greatest discovery of my generation is that human beings can alter their lives by altering their attitudes of mind."[30]

Choose thoughts of faith and expectancy

"You must never be fearful about what you are doing when it is right."

– Rosa Parks

"Our thoughts and expectations wield tremendous power and influence in our lives. We don't always get what we deserve in life, but we usually get no more that we expect; we receive what we believe. Unfortunately, this principle works as strongly in the negative as it does in the positive."[31] Choose faith instead of fear! Expect good things to happen! Occasionally, you will be tempted to think discouraging thoughts, like, "I'm never going to make it; my problems are just too great, they're insurmountable."

Choose each morning to say "good things are going to happen today. It's going to be a great day! I'm excited about today." Expect circumstances to change in your favor. Expect to be in the right place at the right time. Our expectations set the boundaries for our lives.

I recently heard about a young woman who needed emergency surgery and, for some reason, it wasn't covered by her health insurance. Consequently, she owed the hospital $27,000. The hospital worked out a payment plan, and she was paying the bill little by little each month. But she was really struggling. As a single parent, she couldn't afford the extra payment. Nevertheless, she didn't get discouraged. She didn't go around complaining about how tough her life was, or how the hospital had the audacity to charge her so much. Instead she chose to stay in an attitude of faith and expectancy . She continued to keep her emotional frequency high, she continued to expect good things to happen and she continued, on a daily basis, to say to herself:

"It's going to be a great day! I'm excited about today."... Right before Christmas she received a letter from the hospital. The letter basically said, "Every year we like to choose a few families and do something good for them. And this year we've chosen you. We want to inform you that we are canceling your $27,000 debt."

The hospital not only forgave the debt, but also refunded her several thousand dollars that she already paid.[32]

I believe this story illustrates how faith and expectancy resonate with the universal powers of Divine Source - and bring the resolution of problems in ways we can't imagine.

Some people say. "Well, my circumstances have me down. You don't know what I'm going through."

Actually, your circumstances don't have you down. Your thoughts about your circumstances have you down. On the other hand, you can be in one of the biggest battles of your life and still be filled with joy and peace and victory – if you simply lean how to choose the right thoughts.[33]

Choose inspired thoughts

"It is our choices that show what we truly are,
far more than our abilities."

– J.K. Rowling

Choose higher beliefs in your work and life, and you will move Higher Intelligence to work on your behalf. Connection to higher intelligence is inspiration.

When I think of the word inspiration, I like to think of it as meaning "in – spirit," or spiritually minded. That which inspires you, is calling you to take inspired action. It is calling you to move toward what you are intended to be.

When I chose to follow my passion for writing I found that I was also choosing a way of thinking that is guided by inspiration. Writing puts me in a flow state where time doesn't exist and the flood gates of inspiration open wide. When I am in this state I am able to effortlessly write all day long. I don't need to be motivated to do it. The only burden is having to stop while the inspiration is flowing.

By choosing to follow your passion and purpose you will also be choosing to think inspired thoughts. These go hand in hand.

Choose thoughts of abundance

> *"I am no longer cursed by poverty because I took possession of my own mind, and that mind has yielded me every material thing I want, and much more than I need. But this power of mind is a Universal one available to the humblest person as it is to the greatest."*
>
> – Andrew Carnegie

"The word affluence comes from the root word "affluere,' which means "to flow to'. The word affluence means 'to flow in abundance.' Money is really a symbol of the life energy we exchange and the life energy we use as a result of the service we provide to the universe. Another word for money is 'currency,' which also reflects the flowing nature of energy. The word currency comes from the Latin word 'currere' which means "to run" or to flow.[34] Abundance is our divine birthright. Abundance is a connection to God, the source of all abundance. We experience abundance when the Source energy is flowing freely into our lives. We can experience abundance in our relationships, an abundance of health, an abundance of peace and abundance in our finances. The thing that separates us from abundance is the resistance of our limiting beliefs. We will learn more about limiting beliefs in the next chapter.

God's intention for the Children of Israel was for them to have a life of flowing abundance in their land of promise. Universal laws make that same inheritance available to all who seek to align with their Divine Purpose.

Are you facing an area of lack in your life? Lack in your finances, lack in your relationships, lack in your physical health? The good news is that's not the place God wants you to stay. He wants to bring you into a "new land" with no lack, no shortage, no defeat and no mediocrity. He wants you to live in a place where you will have more than enough so you can be a blessing to others. He wants to lift you up and keep you up. He wants you to remain stable and strong in Him.

Why do people want abundance so badly? Their real desire is for the feelings they believe abundance will bring them. It is for the feelings of freedom from fear, stress, anxiety and worry of not having enough and feelings of freedom from having to work so hard to make ends meet. So, in reality, it is the feelings of freedom from painful emotions that they really desire.

The paradox is that the ability to connect with abundance comes after we are free from fear, anxiety and stress about the lack of abundance. In other words, we have to create inner abundance first and then the emotions that accompany inner abundance will resonate with the energy of abundance. If you want to change your outer world you have to change your inner world!

Universal laws state that beliefs, thoughts and emotions always come first. We create outer abundance by means of the abundance we have within.

True Success and abundance flow to us when we are aligned with it. It's not about what we "do," it's about who we "are."

Don't limit the scope of your Divine Purpose with a scarcity mentality. Abundance is all around you, you just have to allow it, by aligning with it.

Wendy Betterini, the creator of the "Allow Abundance Course" has been a sort of mentor to me, in helping me to choose to allow abundance. This is an email I received from her:

"Have you ever had a day where all forms of abundance seemed to be drawn to you? Perfect parking spaces appeared exactly when you needed them, the people you encountered were friendly and helpful, traffic was lighter than usual, you seemed to have plenty of money to do the things you wanted to do, great opportunities showed up with perfect timing, time seemed to slow down so you were able to finish everything on your to-do list quickly and easily, and you just felt good and seemed to attract good wherever you went . . .

For most people, days like this are few and far between. Most often, they feel overwhelmed, stressed, and depleted - mentally, physically, and financially. Does this describe you too?

If so, you'll be interested to know that you have far greater control over your daily life experiences than you realize, and it's very possible to create an ongoing flow of abundance in all forms into your life.

To do this, itis helpful to understand the conditions that repel abundance: Stress, Anxiety, and Anger

When you are tense, stressed, irritated, hurried, harried, overwhelmed, or angry, abundance can't enter your life because you are not a vibrational match to it. The essence of abundance is more aligned with good-feeling emotions like joy, love, appreciation, and relaxation.

Think back to the last smooth, easy day you had, and you'll probably remember that you were in a good mood that day. You felt good, maybe you slept well so you were fully rested, or perhaps you were enjoying a day off from work. In chapter four you'll get a better understanding of why a relaxed, uplifted mindset will always resonate with the good things you desire !

Grasping Desperately

The more you grasp at money and feel desperate and needy for it, the more you repel it. When you are in a desperate, anxious, fearful state of mind, you are not a vibrational match to the essence of abundance, so it can't come to you. When you relax and detach from it emotionally and start appreciating the money you have, affirming that more is on the way, and trusting that all is well, you immediately start allowing more abundance to flow into your life.

Are you seeing a common theme with these causes? They can be boiled down to one simple statement: When you feel good, you are aligned with abundance; when you feel bad, you are aligned with scarcity and struggle.

It really is that simple!"

Wendy Betterini has been teaching and writing about personal development and spiritual topics for more than a decade. She is the author of the Allow Abundance Course, a 26-week "energy makeover" for healing blockages to abundance. See more of Wendy's work at

http://www.allowabundancecourse.com

Key#3 - Choose Emotions that Align with Divine Purpose

"Feelings are much like waves, we can't stop them from coming but we can choose which ones to surf!"

- Unknown

Choose passion

> *"Don't ask yourself what the world needs, ask yourself what makes you come alive. And then go and do that. Because what the world needs is people who are alive."*
>
> – Howard Thurman

Passion is a high-frequency emotion that resonates powerfully with Divine Purpose. Everyone has passions that are unique to them.

Because some people are born with such incredible talents, they are aware of their passions from a very young age. Michelangelo, for instance, knew as a very young boy that he had a passion for sculpting. There are some people who know they were meant to sing and their passion drives them to be on stage sharing their talent with others, but what about people who don't have a talent that allows them to get up on stage and perform?

Your passion is not your Divine Purpose, but it definitely provides clues. Passion is about the process, and Divine Purpose is about the journey.

There is a great price to be paid for not living your passion – the price of living an unfulfilling and uninspired life, the price of not aligning with the flow of True Success!

"Whenever you are faced with a choice, a decision or an opportunity, choose in favor of your passion." - Janet and Chris Atwood

Our Divine Purpose is the intersection of our passion and what we offer the world. One way to determine your passion, though, is discovering what your unique gift to the world is. The passion flows from that.

Many people have a hard time identifying their passions. I think these are a few of the reasons why:

- Our insecurities define us more than our hidden, suppressed dreams.

- We are afraid to boast.
- We see the vastness of the world and feel insignificant or overwhelmed to make a difference.
- We feel it is selfish to become introspective.
- We're extremely busy maintaining an overbooked life and don't have time to reconsider why we're working ourselves to death.
- We think it's wrong to do what we love.
- We felt the sting of rejection the last time we tried operating in our passion, and we've let that rejection scare us.
- We are afraid if we identify it, we'll have to do something, to act on it (and that means risking failure).

Do any of these resonate with you?

I want to share a letter I received.. This woman is an amazing example of someone connecting to divine purpose.

"Dear Randy,

I remember the administrative director at my small college looking straight into my eyes and saying, 'You need to leave college because you cannot afford to stay, your parents can't pay the $458 a month to keep you here and we can't give you any more work study hours to help finance your tuition.' That day was a Wednesday.

By Friday they had changed the locks on my dorm room door, notified the instructors not to allow me in class, and had deactivated my meal pass. I was broke, broken and locked out of college.

I stumbled gracefully over the next ten years. My gift of gab eloquently covered up my fear of failure and of being judged. I kept thinking 'As soon as I stop being scared, I'm gonna really take off. As soon as I get this thing perfect, I'm going to be the bomb dot com.'

Fired from 5 jobs between age 21 and 26, I quickly discovered what I DIDN'T do well. Sitting in an office was not something I was destined for.

Then came along my unexpected God-gift. And 8 months after my son entered our lives, his father whom I had an amazing 13 months of sheer romance and dreaming big with, was sent to prison.

On that day, I made a declaration that by the time that my son graduated from high school that I would be able to support him to live his dreams without lack, scarcity or limitations. That he would NOT have the same experience I had on that Wednesday in that administrator's office.

So as I sit in this town car, on my way to be with my son for the first few days of his journey that starts in Tortola, British Virgin Islands and ends in Italy, this proud mama can say we did it. Living the breathtaking life I intended to have for him and ready to send my son around the world to explore ALL of the possibilities available to him."

All I can say is "Wow!" The human spirit is so powerful. You can't help but notice the incredible passion she feels for life. Even though it may seem risky, do what you are passionate about. Otherwise you will always be chasing after something else until you find what you are passionate about. If you don't pursue your passions, where will you be in one year, five years, and ten years? How will you feel having allowed ten more years of your life to pass doing what you know will not fulfill you? If you can look out ten years and know that you will regret the path you chose, that is the greatest risk of all.

Focus on your passions. We all enjoy doing many different things, but we don't necessarily feel passionate about all of them. You need to figure out which of the things you love doing are things that truly stir your passion – the things you can't get enough of; the things that make you feel so good while you're doing them that you don't want to stop.

People talk all the time about following your passions, but does it just leave you feeling frustrated? If you're struggling with one of these big obstacles, it might. You might want to do what you love, but feel you can't even get started. You might feel overwhelmed, lost, or both. You might feel like you're missing out on all the amazing things you could do, if you just knew where to focus.

What are these obstacles I'm talking about?

"Here they are:

1. Having too many interests and feeling unfocused and scattered all the time.

2. Having no idea where to even begin looking for passions.

These two big problems related to living your passions are actually two sides of the same coin. The problem is actually a lack of focus on the TRUE self.

If you are overwhelmed because you have so many things you love, you feel pulled in 10 different directions and you feel like 9 lives wouldn't be enough to do all the things you want to do, you probably never get anywhere.

When you've lost your compass – the one that points to what's most important to you – you might have lost your sense of direction and get nothing done (or at least nothing that feels like it really means something.) OR, maybe you don't really know what you're passionate about?

Maybe you're so busy with all the responsibilities you have that you never have time for yourself. Perhaps knowing yourself wasn't a priority or a value you grew up with, and only now do you see what it means to not have that.

Rest assured - it's not that your passions don't exist, just that they have been ignored for so long that they're sitting in the corner, sulking until they are coaxed out. At the core, the problem is the same - a disconnection from who you are, and needing to find your way back to YOU.

So what's to be done about it?

The way around these two obstacles is the same. You need to understand YOU. Here are some suggestions for doing that:

1. MAKE time for yourself. Whether you're too busy or it's never been a priority, if you want to find your passions you have to get to know the real you. Make time to get to know your real

self. Schedule it into your calendar (really) and then use it with suggestions below.

2. Tune in. Journal, meditate, find time for quiet. In these moments, thoughts, ideas and images will bubble up from inside. They are telling you something, so pay attention.

3. Experience. If you feel like you don't know where your passions are, make time to experience new things. Take a pottery class, explore fiction writing, join a running club. Find new things that you think you might be interested in and see where it takes you.

4. Consolidate. If you have too many passions, see if they fit into categories. The reason to do this is not because you can't or shouldn't be multi-passionate (you can). But categories may help you to focus on an idea. For example, your love of trail running, photography and birds may point to a passion "category" of enjoying the outdoors. Once you understand that passion, you may be able to focus on it and pursue your path more clearly.

5. Notice. As you go through your day, notice when you're lit up and when you're feeling flat. These peaks and valleys help you notice your passions. You'll discover things you love that you didn't know about before, and you'll discover that some of the things you thought you loved are actually not quite what you expected.

6. Know what your natural talents and skills are. What are you good at? What do you do very well? What are people always asking you to help them with? What things are important to you? Which causes, issues or subjects really get you fired up? On which of these issues would you like to make a difference?

7. Request inspired guidance from your Source of Higher Power! Say something like: "I intend to discover a powerful purpose for my life and I am open to insight and guidance." Or, "I

know you will show me the most perfect purpose for my life, and I know I'm going to love it!" Or, "Please show me the best ways for me to live a purposeful, passionate life."[35]

People who follow their passion are usually those who go the furthest and develop the highest levels of mastery, because of their love for what they do.

Choose gratitude

Choose to focus on what a blessing it is to wake up in the morning and think, "Awesome, I get to follow my passion today!" Gratitude connects us to an infinite power! Be grateful for the blessing of being focused, inspired, and empowered by knowing your Divine Purpose, and progressing in it each day.

Choose Joy

I have experienced for myself that there can be no True Success in life without joy. For many years of my life I was "success-driven," but that drive came from an "outside-in" focus. Joy flows in the opposite direction. It flows from the "inside-out."

True Success begins on the inside. True Success and joy are spiritual in nature. They flow naturally as we align with our Divine Purpose!

The ultimate purpose for which we were created is to have joy! If you are not experiencing joy, choose to rediscover your true self and reconnect to your Divine Purpose.

We all have something inside us that tells when we are not aligned with our purpose. We can gauge our connection to purpose by the amount of joy we experience. The things that bring you the most joy are the things that are most aligned with your purpose. They are what you were created to do and be.

Spend more time doing things that inspire you; things that make your heart sing. The more time you spend on inspiring activities, the higher your frequency will be, and the quicker you will align with your Divine Purpose.

1. Take time every day to experience beauty. Walk in nature, look at sunsets, gaze at stars or whatever makes you experience a sense of beauty, joy and inspiration.

2. Take time every day to do something you are passionate about. Building a career around your passions is the best way to find True Success.

3. Take time every day to love and appreciate people. Spend time just loving the most important people in your life. Accept people as they are and love them for their God-given uniqueness.

4. Always follow your heart and pursue the things that resonate in your soul.

Joy comes by living your life with an inspired purpose. Jack Canfield tells this story of what happened for a young woman named Julie that reconnected with her life's purpose and took inspired action to make a significant change in her life. When Jack met Julie she was about 26 years old. She was a student at Ohio State University. She majored in Veterinary medicine, because everyone had told her that she should become a veterinarian because she loved animals. So she went to the University and began taking courses in biology, biochemistry and anatomy. Soon she realized that she had no interaction with animals, and had no time to spend with her dogs, cats and horses. Then she received a scholarship at a university in Manchester England and after a year realized that she was miserable. She asked herself, "Why am I so miserable, I'm doing what everyone told me to do? I'm studying all of this science, but what I really love is animals, not this." She asked herself, "When was I happiest in my life? When did I experience the most joy?" And what she realized was that she experienced the most joy when she was teaching leadership skills to the students at the university, and when she was a youth leader herself in high school. And she said: "I get it! I'm happiest when I'm involved in leadership.

So she went back to Ohio State and told them: "What I would like to study is leadership, is there a program I can create, because there's not a leadership degree. And they let her do it. She created all the courses. It took her two years longer to graduate, but as a result she graduated with a degree in leadership and when she met Jack at the age of 26 she was working at the Pentagon teaching leadership skills to colonels, admirals and generals. She had become a management consultant in leadership development and leadership training.

She went on to form a foundation called "Role Models and Mentors for Youth Foundation." She was finally back teaching leadership to youth.

By stopping to look at what brought her joy, she was able to reconnect with her true purpose.

If you are not following what resonates for you, you probably are not experiencing joy. We all have things that bring us joy. For me, it is looking at stars, sunrises and sunsets; it is beautiful summer nights, and stunning mountain views. I feel joy when I'm reading and writing inspiring thoughts and insights.

Joy connects you to the energy field that flows from your Source.

The prescription, for connecting with Divine Purpose, is a high dose of joy. Take time every day to experience the things that bring you joy. You feel joy in those things for a reason. Those are the God-given signals that were intended to show you your true self. You were intended to feel joy in things that are part of your Divine Purpose.

The great composer George Frederick Handel began his career as an ego-driven composer who had a "reslessless quest for fame, and public praise"[36] . Handel pursued success in the wrong way - putting fame and fortune as his highest priority. but the trials he experienced prepared him to finally connect to his Divine Purpose: composing The Messiah. As he pursued his self-driven path to success, he endured numerous failures. He pushed himself beyond the limit of his physical capabilities to the point where he eventually suffered a stroke. Handel's doctor stated at the time, "We may save the man, but the musician is lost forever. It seems to me that his brain has been permanently injured."[37] Handel spent the next four months completely unable to speak or move. After those four months of living hell, Handel began to miraculously regain his strength. He joyfully said, "I have come back from Hades."[38] . Yet Handel's return to composing only resulted in further failures, and he became discouraged and despondent. In his despondency he exclaimed, "Why did God permit my resurrection, only to allow my fellow-men to bury me again?"[39]

He was finally asking the right questions. He was finally ready to let go of the ego-driven quest for fame and align with his divine purpose.

One day he was feeling a deep emptiness, and decided to go for a walk. Upon returning home, he found someone had left him a parcel. He discovered it contained a manuscript from a poet by the name of Charles Jennes.

This is how divine purpose works! It is not something we achieve. It is something we choose to connect to. It is something we are intended to become. Handel had not in any way pursued the manuscript. It was delivered to him by his Source! Ego had nothing to do with the creation of this sacred masterpiece; it was given to him through divine inspiration.

The manuscript included verses from the scriptures foretelling the birth of Jesus Christ. As Handel began reading through the text, the first words lept from the page: "Comfort ye." The words seemed to lift the darkness he had been under for so long. His inspiration began to flow, and for the next three weeks he hardly slept or ate as he concluded his work. Upon its completion, he humbly acknowledged, "God has visited me."[40]

Connecting with his Divine Purpose transformed him. He donated the profits from his performances of the Messiah to prisoners, orphans, and the sick. He said, "I have myself been a very sick man, and now am cured. I was a prisoner, and now have been set free." (Ibid   ) Handel had been freed from ego and driven-ness. He had been freed from his relentless quest for fame, fortune, and public praise. He had connected with his divine purpose – his ultimate calling, and in doing so he re-connected with God.

Handel did not create the Messiah in and of himself. He received it into the physical realm through divine inspiration. His Divine Purpose had been fulfilled; he connected with it by means of his "divine obsession"- his joy!

Choose to Let Go of Your Past

You may have suffered much, endured great hardships, or been through a lot of negative things. You may have deep scars from emotional wounds, but don't let your past determine your future. You can't do anything about what's happened to you, but you can choose how you will face what's in front of you.

Let me tell you of a dreamer who let go of his past and found his Divine Purpose

Some of you may not be familiar with the famous T.V show from the sixties, The Andy Griffith Show. There was a character in the show named Barney Fife that was played by the actor Jessie Don Knotts. He played the part of a very small, insecure man who was full of anxiety and nervous twitches and he was hilarious. I always thought he was an amazing actor for the way he played this fearful character, but here is the rest of the story.

Before becoming an actor, Jesse was a chicken plucker. He stood on a line in a chicken factory and spent his days pulling the feathers off dead chickens so the rest of us wouldn't have to. He absolutely hated his job. But he struggled with his beliefs about his own worth and abilities..

Don grew up with a father that was very mean and treated him roughly all of his life.

Don had an older brother who was about the same. He was always picking on him and beating him up. Don's life was definitely not easy. And he thought life didn't hold much hope for him. That's why he was working as a chicken pluckcr, doing a job that few people wanted.

In addition to all the rough treatment at home, Don experienced a lot of illness. Sometimes it was real physical illness, but a lot of it was mental. He was a small, skinny child. That made the situation more difficult..

He was a hypochondriac and that made hima target for bullies. Don didn't believe he had much to look forward to.

But inspite of his problems he still had dreams. He wanted to be a ventriloquist. He found books on ventriloquism. He practiced with sock puppets and saved money until he could get a real ventriloquist dummy.

When he got old enough, he joined the military. And even though many of his hypochondriac symptoms persisted, the military did recognize his talents and put him in the entertainment corp.

That was when his world changed. He gained confidence. He found that he had a talent for making people laugh.

Jesse had found purpose. Instead of overcoming his weakness, he found purpose in it, and become one of the best-loved characters of all time in doing it! He incorporated his nervousness and anxieties into the character he played on television. By being able to embrace his true self, he was able to connect with his amazing talent for humor that had been dormant within. He transferred his nervousness into a successful career and holds the record for the most Emmy's given in a single category.

"No matter where you've been, no matter what you've done, realize today that your destiny supersedes your mistakes. When God designed the

plan for your life, it wasn't dependent on you being perfect, never making a mistake, or never taking a wrong turn. No, God knew we would all make mistakes. He knows how to get you back on track no matter where you are in life. Just like there are many routes on a map, God has a plan to help you reach your destination. He has detours, shortcuts and bypasses. He has already calculated the entire route for your life.

Today, if you're feeling like you've blown it, if you feel like you are too old, too far gone or too off track, know that nothing you've done, no mistake that you've made — or ever will make — is a surprise to God. He's already got it figured out. He's arranged a comeback for every setback! He has grace for every weakness. He has mercy for every failure. Receive it today and move forward with boldness into the destiny He has for you!"
– Joel Osteen

There are many people who feel like they've wasted years of their lives because of poor choices. They have spent years in bad relationships, years trapped in addiction, years stuck in jobs where they weren't fulfilled. But you have to realize, nothing you have been through is ever wasted.

All of these experiences have prepared you to embrace your Divine Purpose. Your Divine Purpose will connect you with the right people, the right opportunities, and the right circumstances to move you forward toward your God-given destiny.

Don't focus on what has happened in your past. Focus on your future of Divine Purpose. Alignment with your Divine Purpose will restore your soul and revive your dreams. Keep believing, keep expecting, and keep hoping because your Divine Purpose has a new direction for your life!

Choose to Let Go of Anxiety

Anxiety could be called a "killer" in general terms because of its detrimental effects on our health and well-being, but did you know it can also kill prosperity before it ever reaches you?

Prosperity is nothing more than a flow of beneficial energy through your life. This flow of energy can take the form of monetary wealth (which is what we usually imagine in terms of prosperity), but it also includes things like love, happiness, peace, fulfillment, and joy. When you are tense and anxious, you automatically constrict this energy from flowing freely through your life!

Imagine a flexible tube through which water flows. If you grasp the tube and squeeze it, you decrease the flow or cut it off entirely. When you relax your grip (ease the constriction) the water flows freely again.

Anxiety does the same thing to the flow of purpose, inspiration, vision, and prosperity into your life.

We will discuss techniques for countering this in the next chapter.

Key# 4 – Choose Actions That Align With Divine Purpose

Your words and actions are the fruits of your emotions. And remember, it is your emotions that send out your signal.

Words can begin as tiny seeds. But as you speak them aloud, they become planted in your subconscious minds, and begin to take on a life of their own; they take root, grow and produce more of the same kind of fruit. If you speak positive words, your life will move in that direction. Similarly, negative words will produce poor results. You can't speak words of defeat and failure and expect to live in victory.

When you say something often enough, with enthusiasm and passion, before long your subconscious mind begins to act on what you are saying, doing whatever is necessary to bring those thoughts and words to pass. This is where "I am" statements come in. Whenever you say the words: "I am" followed by a positive or negative statement about yourself the subconscious mind accepts it as a fact. We will discuss the power of "I am" statements in principle five.

If you are struggling with low self-esteem, you need to go overboard in speaking positive, faith-filled words of victory about yourself and your life. Here are a few examples:

- I am excited about my future!
- I am aligned with my Higher Purpose!
- I am experiencing the goodness of God!
- I am loving life today!
- I am attracting everything I need for success!

If you want to connect to Divine Purpose, stop talking about how big your problems are and start talking about the things you want to see manifesting in your life.

Begin speaking words of faith over your life. "Your words have enormous creative power. The moment you speak something out, you give birth to it. This is a spiritual principle, and it works whether what you are saying is good or bad, positive or negative."[41]

Choose to surround yourself with greatness

Choose to surround yourself with high-energy people! Choose friends who are full of faith, friends who think positively and speak words that plant good fruit. Choose people who are sowing seeds of greatness in their lives and making a difference in the world. Choose to reach out to positive people who will support and nurture you in your dreams and passions.

Coming from a sales background, I was taught by my sales manager the 80/20 rule. In sales this means that 80% of your sales will come from the top 20% of your customers. It also held true that in any sales force 80% of the sales will be made by the top 20% of the sales people. This rule seems to be true in almost all aspects of life. The chances are that about 20% of the people in your life are producing 80% of your enjoyment and opportunities for growth. There is another 20% that are causing 80% of your depression, anger and second guessing.

We spend too much time with those who poison us with pessimism, sloth and low expectations of themselves and the world. Drop them like a bad habit.

Choose Mentors

Choose successful people to coach you and support you through the learning curves that need to be experienced. You want the counsel and advice of people who have already accomplished the things your divine purpose is calling you to do, but in the end when a decision has to be made, you need to follow your heart and do what resonates. If something does not feel right, that is dissonance. It is a signal that the action you are considering is not in alignment with your Divine Purpose.

Choose to Serve

Have you heard the phrase, "Give and you shall receive?" That is a perfect demonstration of the energy exchange that takes place when you start following your purpose. Your purpose doesn't affect just you. It affects everyone who comes into contact with your works, whatever they may be.

Make a transition from a place of ambition to a place of mission. Mission always focuses outward on serving and adding value to the lives of others, but ambition focuses solely on self+

When you create something or provide a service, you are sharing a part of yourself with the world (or even just a small part of the world), and that positive energy you send out will come back in a beneficial form. It might be money, it might be gratitude, it might be joy, or other forms of abundance.

The thing to remember about a passionate purpose – whatever you have to offer the world, someone out there needs it and wants it!

As long as you stay focused on a positive outcome for your purpose, you will attract the clients, the customers, the business partnerships, the funding, the location, the resources and inventory . . . whatever you need to make your purpose a living, breathing reality.

Choose to Surrender and Allow

> *"Just trust that everything is unfolding the way it is supposed to. Don't resist. Surrender to what is, let go of what was, and have faith in what will be. Great things are waiting for you around the corner."*
>
> - Sonia Ricotti

Having made choices to follow your dreams and passions, now choose to remain detached. Often we get a preconceived notion of how we think our dreams will manifest, and many times it manifests a little differently than we thought.

Ask yourself, "If this dream of mine doesn't manifest, how will I feel?" Frustrated? Disillusioned? Disappointed?

If you are not detached you will feel anxious, wondering, "What if it doesn't work?"

Instead ask yourself, "Is there still something purposeful intended for my future?"

If you're too attached to something, you're giving up your control over how you feel, so you have to let go of thinking: "It has to happen or I'll feel like a failure." Your dreams will never manifest that way!

You need a mindset of: "This or something better is coming my way." Just be excited that something great is coming.

Total surrender means accepting the fact you don't know the answers consciously, you can't imagine the answer. In the next chapter we'll discuss the different levels of brain-wave activity, but for now just accept that without surrender, you are stuck in a state of mind that doesn't have full access to the higher intelligence of your Sourcewhich knows your Divine Purpose and what is best for you.

You must learn to align with Universal laws. Allow, don't control! Remember if you are creating a signal of anxiety, fear and stress you will resonate with more of the same.

"Success is not final, Failure is not fatal, it is the courage to continue that counts."
— Winston Churchill

Whatever you do, don't allow yourself to be overcome by confusion, fear, and doubt. You don't have to have all of the answers right now. Just stay focused on what you want to happen, even if you aren't clear on all of the details. You will be led to the fulfillment of your deepest, biggest dreams if you just have faith and patience and take one step at a time.

Right now you may have the belief that a purposeful life can't be created easily, especially if your life seems very far from purposeful right now. Get rid of that belief! Universal laws, if tapped into correctly, offer unlimited powers for our benefit, and you can activate those by simply trusting that the process can be easy and smooth.

Let go and let Divine Intelligence work! Surrendering your life and your work to higher purposes gives it the winning edge. In an infinite, abundant universe, we needn't fear that surrender leads to loss; it is in fact the key to gain.

I don't doubt that there are plenty of hard, strenuous, unpleasant ways to transform your life into something more purposeful, but I also know that there are even more wonderful, enjoyable, effortless ways to achieve the same thing. Your job is to focus on allowing those smooth, easy circumstances to unfold before you. If you expect it to be easy and fun, it will be.

Because we've all been taught to "work hard," what we end up doing is paddling up stream and not getting anywhere. Instead, we need to learn to relax into the process, to trust in our inner guidance and start taking the actions where it makes sense. Then we must pay attention to the feedback. The feedback will say, "Wait, this feels too hard, this feels effortful and painful. Pain is an indicator that something's off course. So you have to look back and say, "where is the flow, where is the easy part?"

You have to start surrendering to this feeling called flow. Trust the process and everything will unfold.

Your Divine Purpose has been planted in your soul. Your job now is to allow it to emerge.

The belief that you really have to work harder is shooting you in the foot. Why do we feel like we need to work hard? Is it to try and make it happen? How is it working out? The very effort that we put forth can send a dissonant signal of tension, struggle and anxiety. Do any of our desperate efforts keep the world in its orbit? Our fanatical efforts are often the very things that hold us back. You were put into this world to joyously create!

What if the source of divine energy that keeps all things in balance was supporting the things that you desire to create? That divine energy makes all the needed resources available to you.

When we submit to a Higher Purpose we experience the flow of divine help. When we know we are in alignment, burdens are lifted, although we may not fully know where we are headed.

Choose to Eliminate Ego

Biblical teachings state that "with God all things are possible." So if all we see are impossibilities, our energy signal will be dissonant from Source Energy and our Divine Purpose.

Our true self is ONE with God, ONE with others and ONE with all of God's creations. Success myths keep us in a false sense of self that isn't aligned with a Higher Power and they keep us from allowing our Divine Purpose to emerge. Thus, they are rooted in ego. We could say that ego stands for Edging God Out. Ego is the idea that we are somehow separate from our Divine Source. It causes us to see ourselves as separate from the flow of Divine energy. It causes us to see ourselves in terms of what is missing in our lives. When we are caught up in ego, we choose to identify ourselves in terms of our possessions and our accomplishments. Ego is a false sense of self. It drives us to compete and compare, especially in terms of material possessions. Ego fears the concept of aligning with a Higher Power, because it sees spiritual things as foolishness.

Ego cannot coexist with our Divine Purpose. Ego is temporary and always changing while our Divine Purpose is permanent. When we move away from ego; we move into an inspired knowing that "all things are possible."

Here are some famous quotes that demonstrate the human tendency toward ego-based limiting beliefs:

- *"The more important fundamental laws and facts of physical science have all been discovered, and these are now so firmly established that the possibility of their ever being supplanted in consequence of new discoveries is exceedingly remote.... Our future discoveries must be looked for in the sixth place of decimals."*-- Albert. A. Michelson, German-born American physicist, 1894

- *"I think there is a world market for maybe five computers."*-- Thomas Watson, chairman of IBM, 1943

- *"There is no reason anyone would want a computer in their home."*-- Ken Olson, president, chairman and founder of Digital Equipment Corp. (DEC), maker of big business mainframe computers, arguing against the PC, 1977

- *"A rocket will never be able to leave the Earth's atmosphere."*-- New York Times, 1936 ("Who the hell wants to hear actors talk?"-- H.M. Warner, Warner Brothers, maker of silent movies, 1927

- *"There is no likelihood man can ever tap the power of the atom."*-- Robert Millikan, American physicist and Nobel Prize winner, 1923

- *"Airplanes are interesting toys but of no military value."*-- Marechal Ferdinand Foch, Professor of Strategy, Ecole Superieure de Guerre, 1904(?)

- *"The horse is here to stay, the automobile is only a fad."*-- Advice of President of Michigan Savings Bank to Horace Rackham, lawyer for Henry Ford, 1903 (Rackham ignored the advice and invested $5000 in Ford stock, selling it later for $12.5 million.

- *"Heavier-than-air flying machines are impossible."*-- Lord Kelvin, British mathematician and physicist, president of the British Royal Society, 1895

- *"We are probably nearing the limit of all we can know about astronomy."*-- Simon Newcomb, Canadian-born American astronomer, 1888

- *"Well-informed people know it is impossible to transmit the voice over wires and that were it possible to do so, the thing would be of no practical value."*-- Boston Post, 1865

- *"Television won't last because people will soon get tired of staring at a plywood box every night."*-- Darryl Zanuck, movie producer, 20th Century Fox, 1946

- *"Rail travel at high speeds is not possible because passengers, unable to breathe, would die of asphyxia."*-- Dionysius Lardner, Professor of Natural Philosophy and Astronomy at University College, London, and author of The Steam Engine Explained and Illustrated, 1830s

- *"...so many centuries after the Creation it is unlikely that anyone could find hitherto unknown lands of any value."*-- Committee advising King Ferdinand and Queen Isabella of Spain regarding a proposal by Christopher Columbus, 1486

So far we've discussed the principles of resonance, energy and agency and how they give us the power to choose a connection to our Divine Purpose. In principle four we will take a deeper look at the universal principle of mind renewal and how to renew our connection to Divine Intelligence when it is clouded with fears, doubts and limiting beliefs.

The purpose of reprograming your conscious mind is to change your focus and raise the frequency of your thoughts and emotions, but it is only the beginning. The fastest way to make changes to our resistance is to turn our focus to the "software of the soul" - your subconscious blueprint. The programming of your subconscious mind determines your ability to have a free-flowing connection to Higher Power.

Summary
How do I apply this principle?

- Ask, believe and receive
- Choosing responsibility for your beliefs, thoughts and action

Benefits

- Realize you have the power to change your frequency
- Experience a higher vibrational frequency
- Experience more gratitude, joy and passion
- Experience the flow of Divine Energy

Consequences

- Remain in low-frequency thoughts and emtions
- Remain dissonant

CHAPTER FOUR

How to Reprogram your Subconscious Mind for True Success! Principle #4: Mind Renewal

"Divine Purpose means getting 'who you think you are' aligned with 'who you truly are.'

One day while searching on the internet, I came across a great blog titled: healyourlife.com/blogs. It was there that I found the Story of David Ji.

Without being aligned with who you truly are, you will experience what David Ji referred to as "sleepwalking through life." David worked for many years in the worlds of finance and business in the corporate world of New York City. He had worked on one of the higher floors of Tower Two, at what is now referred to as Ground Zero. One day he realized that his life was spinning out of physical and emotional balance and he realized that he had stopped his practice of meditation. He had replaced his 5 A.M. meditation time with an early morning train ride into the bowels of the World Trade Center, and he had replaced his evening meditation with a double scotch. And suddenly his daily practice of meditation had disappeared.

He noticed that he had lost the balance and deep fulfillment he had once felt during his meditation days. He found himself living to work, to fill an empty part of himself that he had forgotten. It had been many years since he had been able to sleep through the night. Instead, he often awoke at about 2 A.M. with a painful knot in his stomach that stayed there through the day and into the evening. He brought it to bed with him every night. He ate his lunch at his desk while texting and chatting on his cell phone, typing e-mails, and inhaling his sandwich . . . all in five minutes. He realized that he had been doing that for almost 15 years.

Nonstop, overwhelming thoughts relentlessly raced through his head as he attempted to juggle so many different pieces of his life and finding unfulfillment at every turn. He craved peace of mind. He craved his Divine Purpose!. He craved the depth of feeling he had once known in my youth. He felt like he was light-years from that time in his life. He was sleepwalking through his life. His personal and work relationships were stressed and strained. He was waking up, burning through the day, performing his "job," coming home, eating dinner, reading a book or watching TV, and passing out. Sound familiar?

His personal and home lives had been taken over by his career. And his career had been taken over by an autopilot existence. He was empty, adrift from any guiding principle, deeply in pain, purposeless, and unenlightened about what his life had become and where it was headed. He started to question his accomplishments and the value he contributed to others in his life.

And so one day while he was in SoHo, he walked past a row of cardboard boxes in which homeless people were living, a hand reached out and grabbed his pant leg, and a curious, soot-covered face peered up at him and asked, "What's gonna be on your tombstone?" David stopped in his tracks, as his gaze narrowed on the man's blue eyes, and reflected on his life.. Face to face, soul to soul—connected in a transcendent moment, that took his breath away. He felt he was staring into the face of God.

Tears came to his eyes as he was locked in a gaze for what seemed like eternity. As he mouthed the words to the stranger, "I don't know," his mind was a tsunami of thoughts, memories, and desires. He wandered aimlessly for hours after that, the stranger's words reverberating through every cell in his body. He asked himself, what was going to be on his tombstone? What was his purpose? He felt like a prisoner living eternally on death row, stuck in an existence with no purpose.

His mind was now overflowing with images of the collapse of Tower Two, just blocks south of the downtown office building, where he and his staff had stood on the roof and watched in horror on that fateful day. This was a wake-up call, a deep reminder of his need to live a purpose-driven life. But he was light-years from knowing what that purpose was or having it actualized .

That night, as he shared his day's experience with my wife over dinner, she handed him a piece of paper. She had sensed his daily pain and had explored a few deeper options for me to consider. One was Seduction of Spirit, a meditation retreat in England with Deepak Chopra. She encouraged him to follow his heart. A work colleague advised him to:, "Jump and the net will appear." One of his yoga teachers suggested, "Quit your job today. The universe will provide."

David followed his heart and jumped.

One week later, he learned his meditation mantra; one month later, his job evaporated into the ether; and two months later, David headed off to Oxford to meet Deepak Chopra and learn about the concept of dharma—His purpose in life. It was there he learned that the word guru is a Sanskrit term for "remover of darkness," essentially one who teaches enlightenment. But no one else can actually make you "see." They can help you to open and awaken to what already rests within; essentially giving you permission to access aspects of yourself you had previously not given yourself permission to awaken.

Maybe you didn't know they were there. Maybe you did but were unsure how to access them. But once you do awaken to the stillness and silence that rest beneath the layers of activity in your daily life, you will know it's there and forever available to you. Each day, when your meditation is over, you will be able to "listen" to life with greater appreciation and understanding and to live your life with greater grace and ease.

(http://www.healyourlife.com/author-davidji/2012/09/wisdom/ inspiration/are-you-sleepwalking-through-your-life)

No matter what you've been through or where you find yourself currently, the "universal principle of renewal" provides hope that your connection to Divine Purpose can be repaired and strengthened.

As I began trying to live these principles and trying to choose thoughts and emotions that align with True Success, I was running into doubts and fears. My conscious efforts to apply the principles were not enough, because my subconscious mind was resisting. In this chapter we look at how to "renew your mind for True Success" by eliminating the barrier of mental dissonance.

It may take a few months of repetition using the techniques in this chapter to change your neural pathways. The resources on my website may be very helpful. You can access those at <u>www.principlesofdivinepurpose.com</u>.

In this principle you will come to understand more deeply why the success myths we discussed in Principle One cannot lead to True Success. You'll also begin to see the mindset from which these myths sprang.

In the Old Testament there is an interesting example of this principle. When the people of Israel were camped right next door and excited about possessing the land, Moses sent twelve men to spy out the Promised Land. But after 40 days, ten of the men came back with a negative report. They said, "Moses, there are giants in the land, and we'll never defeat them." That negative report spread throughout the rest of the camp, and the people began to murmur and complain.

But one of the spies named Caleb said, "Moses, we are well able to defeat these people. Let us go up at once and take the land!"

It's interesting that they all saw the same land, the same circumstances; yet, they had totally different views. How could their reports be so opposite? Here's how: Caleb had a different spirit. He saw things with a different perspective. Others were focused on the giants, but Caleb was focused on Divine Purpose. The people who complained never actually made it into the Promised Land, but Caleb did. He accompanied a new generation that chose the blessing of God.

God has a Land of Promise prepared for each of us; arriving in that land is our Divine Purpose! But He allows us to wander in wildernesses until we are ready to apply the keys of True Success by choosing to apply Universal Truths. True Success is our heritage, but it requires a renewing of our minds. In this chapter you'll learn how to "renew your mind" in ways that will create greater bandwidth in your connection to your Divine Source.

> *"Out of clutter find simplicity. From discord find harmony. In the middle of difficulty lies opportunity."*
>
> — Albert Einstein

To align with your Divine Purpose you need to stop and "be still." Focus on Divine help and the flow of Divine Purpose. This is especially true during times of difficulty.

Remember, our battles are spiritual battles, so let the battles you face belong to your Higher Power.

The more closed we are in heart, mind and spirit and the narrower our focus and belief systems are, the smaller our lens of perception, and therefore the more limited our playing field is! There is so much more available to us than we realize. To access more options, we simply have to shift and expand the lens through which we view the world, expand our overall perspective on what's possible AND remember that we are infinite beings that are temporarily housed in these physical bodies -- and we have so much dormant potential just waiting to be accessed and realized!

We can create a new foundation for our lives that is broader and more expansive than ever before. The more space we create within our hearts and minds to love and accept and allow for greater options to show up---the more we step into a new magical, miraculous flow that is filled with new options, opportunities that reflect the beauty and magnificence of our soul!

Renew your Mind!

> *"Be not conformed to this world: but be ye transformed by the renewing of your mind, that ye may prove what is that good, and acceptable, and perfect, will of God."*
>
> (Romans 12:2)

Eliminate Subconscious Resistance

Being "conformed to the world," means having a mindset that restricts the flow of inspiration, reducing our ability to see limitless possibilities.

The "renewing of our minds" is the process of eliminating our subconscious resistance that restricts the flow of possibility.

In the telecommunications world they use the term "bandwidth" to describe the capacity of a conduit to allow the 'flow" of information from one place to another. I think bandwidth applies to our connection to Divine Source. The degree of True Success you experience is directly related to the capacity of your bandwidth.

The objective of eliminating subconscious resistance is to develop a bandwidth that transmits a massive signal of faith, gratitude, love, joy and abundance. In turn we receive from our source a massive, effortless flow of enabling power and divine strength. In this way we live our Divine Purpose and experience True Success.

So what limits our bandwidth to True Success?

- Limiting beliefs
- Habitual thinking patterns
- Brain chemistry

Reticular Activating System

The Reticular Activating System (RAS) is a bundle of nerves that sits at the bottom of our brain. It acts as a gate keeper between the conscious and subconscious minds. The conscious mind processes about 40 bits of information a second, but the subconscious mind processes 40 million bits of information per second. That's why people who are in shock after a car wreck don't remember a thing, but under hypnosis they can recall every little detail, because hypnosis accesses the subconscious mind.

The subconscious mind is running the show most of the time. The RAS takes those 40 million bits of information that my subconscious is processing and filters it, allowing into my conscious mind only that which is relevant to my focus. What you focus on determines what the RAS allows into your conscious awareness. With the law of attraction, once you have focused on what you want, visualized yourself already in possession of it, with emotion, and taken action in the direction of your goal, the universe steps in, and you begin to attract all the people, the resources, the ideas and the opportunities you need to achieve it.

The RAS is what helps you recognize those things that the Universe is sending your way to help you achieve your goals and align with your Higher Purpose.

Mind Renewal gives you the tools to change your mindset and renew your connection to your Higher Purpose by raising your frequency! Raising your vibrational frequency is hard for some people to do, but there are techniques that can help you master it. Once you're doing it consistently, you'll begin experiencing a sense of High Purpose.

In order to raise your frequency you can ask yourself, "What would make me feel good right now?"

Feeling good is "feeling God" and learning to raise your frequency is about learning how to tap into the energy that flows from God, the source of universal energy.

Did you have a negative reaction when I asked, "What would make me feel good right now?" Did you immediately think, "That's self-centered" or "Not everything that feels good, is good"?

Remember, this book is about your Divine Purpose not about satisfying your ego or base desires. As you increase your ability to feel good mentally, emotionally and spiritually, you are also increasing your ability to connect with your Divine Source. This means learning techniques that nurture you, uplift you, honor you, and strengthen your spiritual connection.

Actions that only satisfy physical desires like overeating, abusing your body, or being hurtful to other people, may feel satisfying temporarily, but they lower your frequency because of the negative emotions such as guilt, shame and inadequacy that they produce after the temporary pleasure subsides. This only creates more dissonance with your Divine Purpose.

We are referring to the deeper feelings of the spirit, not the shallow feelings of ego. Mind renewal is about re-connecting to spirit, to Divine Purpose and to True Success!

You can make a list and examine all your limiting beliefs. Often these beliefs were created very early in life. If you have focused on limiting beliefs long enough, your brain actually formsneural pathways that align with those beliefs. Later in this principle we'll discuss how those neural pathways set you up in self-destructive habits and compulsions.

If the dreams and passions related to your Divine Purpose aren't manifesting yet, it's not because Universal laws are holding them back from you; it is because you are not yet resonating with them.

Story of Roger Bannister

Only a few decades ago, track-and-field experts believed that breaking the four-minute-mile barrier was an absolute impossibility. They claimed that the human body was not able to do it. They claimed "no human being could run that far, that fast, for that length of time." They even conducted studies to try and prove their assumption. And for many years, they were right. No one was able to run a mile in less than four minutes.

But eventually a young man came along who refused to harbor limiting beliefs. He refused to think in terms of impossibilities. He refused to allow negative thoughts to have a place in his mind. As he began training, he planted in his mind the belief that he was going to break the record. And he did it; he did what people said couldn't be done. His name was **Roger Bannister**, and his name has gone down in sports history.

Here is the most interesting thing about what Roger Bannister accomplished. Ten years later, 336 other runners had also broken the four-minute-mile barrier. Isn't that amazing! For as long as track-and-field records have been kept, nobody had run a mile in less than four minutes; now, within a decade, more than three hundred people have been able to do it as well.

This goes to show that the barrier was not a physical barrier, but a mental one. When the mind is not convinced that something is possible it creates an energy that is dissonant to the thing to be accomplished.[42]

Roger Bannister eliminated the dissonance of a limiting belief for all the athletes who would follow him.

"Whatever you hold in your mind becomes your reality in time. If you change your state of mind, it will change your reality" - Brett Olsen

The most potent energy interrupters in existence are our beliefs, thoughts and emotions. Whether they are empowering or disempowering, true or false, they create a resonance - a vibration that gets mirrored back into our lives.

How to Transform Limiting Beliefs
Limiting beliefs are self-created

Do you have a glass ceiling over your level of success? If so, there are obstacles deep inside you that are holding you back. These obstacles are limiting beliefs. These beliefs are acting as opposing intentions that block your true manifestations from manifesting.

First, let's get clear about what limiting beliefs really are. A belief is nothing more than a thought you have focused on and reinforced dozens and dozens of times – so it eventually becomes your "truth." Your beliefs are neural pathways that have been habitually formed, but they can be changed. A limiting belief is a self-created "truth" that prevents you from following your dreams and manifesting your deepest desires. In other words, it is an obstacle that stands between you and your Divine Purpose.

The important thing to remember is that limiting beliefs are "self-created"? They are! The seeds for some of your limiting beliefs might have been planted in your mind by other people, but you ultimately nurtured them and allowed them to blossom in your life, even if you did it subconsciously.

Whether they originated from your own negative thoughts, or from someone else's influence, they amount to the same thing: they are inner obstacles that will hold you back from the life you are intended for.

Identify limiting beliefs

Before you can change your limiting beliefs, you need to know what they are. But the trouble with most limiting beliefs is that they are subconscious. You rarely, if ever, think about them consciously, but they run silently in the background, influencing your thoughts, feelings, and actions.

Here is an exercise that will help you identify some of your limiting beliefs. On a piece of paper, write the words: "I would like to ________________ (write in the thing that you most desire). At the end of that statement, write the word, "but." Then insert the reasons why it can't be done.

Here is an example. "I would like to write a book about Divine Purpose, but I'm not famous enough for people to want to buy it.

Continue to write out a list of all the things that come to mind.

- No one would want to read anything I wrote.

- It would be way too hard!

- I'm not knowledgeable enough to do that

- I'm not an expert.

- I don't know where to start.

Change Limiting Beliefs

Remember that a belief is nothing more than a self-created "truth" – a thought that you have continued to focus on and reinforce, sometimes for years.But it won't take years to clear your limiting beliefs. If you're very consistent with your efforts, you can change a limiting belief in days – maybe a few weeks for extremely strong beliefs.

What is mind renewal? Basically it is the elimination of limiting beliefs and lies that keep us dissonant from our Divine Purpose. As you change your beliefs, your thoughts will change, and as you change what you think about, your emotions will follow suit. Your emotions ultimately determine the energy frequency that you'll transmit. The *renewing of your mind* is like the changing of a TV channel. With a new frequency an entirely different picture appears! This is what happens when you tune into the frequency of your Divine Purpose.

How is the mind renewed? Before we jump into the actual techniques, let's discuss the power of the subconscious mind.

The Key to Unlimited Bandwidth - Your Subconscious

"There are deeper levels to the Law of Resonance. That which resonates in your life is not based on what you consciously think about. That which resonates is based on your unconscious beliefs."

Eliminate Subconscious Resistance

We increase our mental bandwidth as we get our subconscious beliefs on board with our conscious desires and goals.

When we have both parts of our mind working together it becomes our pipeline to the flow of True Success. When or subconscious beliefs are on-board with our conscious goals there is no resistance and the bandwidth to source energy becomes enormous. The more we can expand our bandwidth the more "flow" we experience and the more we will experience an effortless flow of success. Increased flow comes through increased bandwidth.

Neural dissonance is a form of resistance that reduces our bandwidth. It occurs when there is not alignment between the conscious and subconscious mind. It stops us from "seeing" possibilities. It stops us from resonating with Divine Purpose.

When Napoleon Hill was finishing his book "Think and Grow Rich," he had an experience that demonstrates the powerful bandwidth our subconscious minds possess. As he was struggling to come up with the right title for his book, his publisher finally gave him a one-day deadline in which to come up with a title or they would do it for him.

Before retiring that night, he actually sat in bed and began having a conversation with his subconscious mind. He asked his subconscious mind to reveal to him the title that was intended for the book.

He went to bed and quickly fell asleep, but in the early hours of the morning a flash of inspiration awakened him, and he knew at that moment that the title of his book was to be "Think and Grow Rich."

The subconscious is where the brain and Divine Intelligence connect; kind of like a connection to some sort of spiritual internet. Spirit always operates by law and it always operates perfectly. If your subconscious is filled with limiting beliefs it will affect you spiritually, by making you dissonant to things of the spirit.

All of us would like to make changes in our lives, such as feeling happier, having more meaning and joy on a daily basis, having more financial abundance, losing weight, having better relationships, starting a new career, or taking up a new hobby. But actually making those changes can often be the hard part. Why is that?

The difficulty lies in the fact that our minds are made up of two parts. One part is responsible for rational, conscious thought and processes ideas sequentially, using language. The other part is emotional and processes ideas simultaneously, using pictures.

The emotional, subconscious mind is far more powerful than the rational, conscious mind. It is capable of processing more information, it controls approximately 95 percent of the thoughts you think and the actions you take each day, and is motivated by the pull of pleasurable rewards and the push of negative emotions.

"If you think of the emotional mind as an *elephant* and the rational mind as the *rider*, you can understand the challenge of change. The rider can control the elephant, as long as the elephant doesn't have any strong desires about the direction it wants to go. If the elephant doesn't want to go, the rider has very little chance of forcing it."[43]

Unfortunately, success myths cause us to have an "outside-in" focus as the way to change our lives. Studies have shown that when you attempt to use willpower to create change, success is very limited. Willpower has proven to be an exhaustible resource. Trying to change our lives through willpower alone is like trying to tame the elephant to obey the will of the rider.

If our emotional, subconscious elephant is experiencing fear, anger, sadness, or anxiety, the rider's will is pretty insignificant. We are often quick to blame our inability to make changes on a lack of willpower, moral failing or weakness. But in reality it's just the way our brains are wired.

The beliefs in your subconscious mind actually change what you see in the world, how you reason, and how you figure things out. If you subconsciously believe that you live in lack, or there are no opportunities available to you, you won't be able to see them even if they are right before your eyes. On top of that, because you are focused on "the lack of opportunity," that is what will be attracted to you.

The elephant's limiting beliefs keep it paralyzed, believing not only that success is impossible, but any attempts to try could cause intense pain. Apparently Roger Bannister had an exceptional elephant.

Simply understanding your fears and limiting beliefs, does not give you the ability to overcome them. Consider a person with a fear of flying: He may know consciously that flying is safer than driving in a car. Nevertheless, this doesn't prevent his subconscious mind (elephant) from experiencing symptoms of fear every time he boards an aircraft.

Our minds constantly experience subconscious thoughts that we are not aware of, yet they have a huge effect on our emotions and consequently the vibrational signal that we send out. Our subconscious mind will create for us and attract to us those circumstances that it believes in the present moment.

Success myths are based on the false assumption that our conscious mind (our rider) controls the degree of success we experience, when in reality it is our subconscious mind (our elephant) that determines our success.

The Subconscious Connects to Divine Intelligence.

So how can you know that these Universal laws really exist, other than relying on an inner feeling that it is true? You can know of the reality of these laws by the Universe's responsiveness. These laws work all the time, and the way you align with the power by which they operate is through the power of the subconscious mind.

We are all inherently limited in what we can manifest from our conscious minds, and our subconscious blueprint is going to determine the direction of our life, unless we go in and change it. This is why I was stuck, and no matter how hard I worked or how many personal development books I read. The subconscious programming of my childhood was keeping me stuck, ineffective and victimized in spite of my conscious attempts to focus on success.

Only by changing our subconscious blueprint can we gain the ability to direct our energy in the direction we want it to go. This allows our subconscious attention to give us everything we need for True Success. When our subconscious energy is going in the direction of our dreams and passions, life becomes easy, effortless and we enter the flow state, where there is no need for willpower, there is no forcing and no unpleasantness.

The Gatekeeper

The Gatekeeper, is different from the RAS, but performs a similar function. The Gatekeeper is a filter that stands between the conscious and unconscious minds, or we could say, s between our outer and inner worlds. It rejects information that doesn't match our blueprint. It is designed to keep things the same and be a defense mechanism against fear, doubt and worry. It is the same mechanism that rejects the idea of jumping off a building. It also rejects all other options that would take you out of your subconscious comfort zones.

Most people try to change through willpower and the reality is that willpower doesn't work. It is only our conscious attention overriding our subconscious programming. This can only be temporary. Eventually our conscious attention will slip and our subconscious programming will take over. When we try to change through willpower we are using the wrong part of your mind. We have to bypass the gatekeeper in order to make positive changes in our lives. It is like opening the window inside your mind so that your conscious mind can command the subconscious mind to rewrite the current blueprint.

Our subconscious mind is not limited by time or space and it has the potential to be in direct contact with Divine Intelligence. Our subconscious has two access points. It can be open to instructions from the conscious mind, once we get past the gatekeeper (filter), and it can be open to Higher Intelligence as our bandwidth is expanded through the elimation of limiting beliefs.

Your Subconscious Mind knows your Divine Purpose and it will give you solutions that are aligned with that purpose. When this happens you can't go wrong. This is where the principle of resonance really kicks in.

Techniques to Increase Your Mental Bandwidth

> *"Within you, there is a destiny waiting to be born -- a life of such purpose, creativity and contribution that its light would blind you if apprehended it in its fullness. But to actualize it, you must dive beneath the surface tension of the mind's need to control the present."*
>
> – Derek Rydall

We can increase our mental bandwidth to Divine Intelligence and Source energy as we get our subconscious minds on board with our conscious desires and goals.

Years ago, I worked as a sales representative for a national fundraising company that had a sales force of about 220 sales people. At the time, the most prestigious sales award the company offered was "the Quarter Million Dollar Club." At that time only about 5 or 6 people had ever reached that level of sales. It was considered a very prestigious group to be in and they were rewarded with a nice all-expense paid trip for each sales representative and their spouse. They were also awarded a burgundy blazer at the national awards banquet. It was a big deal.

Even though I had no idea how it would be possible, I had made the decision that I was going to make it into the club the upcoming year. In order to accomplish it, I would need to realize a huge increase over my current level of sales. Fortunately, my mentor understood a little about the subconscious mind and how affirmations, emotions and

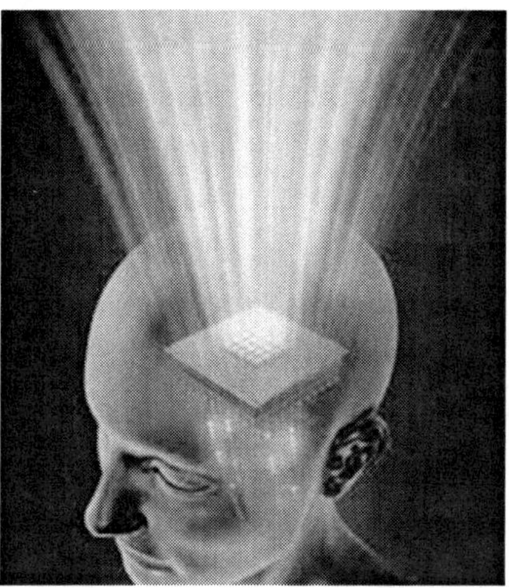

visualization effect our beliefs. He helped me write out affirmations that I kept with me to review continuously. He took pictures of me in the burgundy blazer so I could visually see myself wearing it.

He taught me that the subconscious mind doesn't know the difference between something that is real, and something that is imagined.

As I made use of these tools on a daily basis my subconscious mind began to accept the fact that I was in reality a member of the club, and it went to work connecting me with all the ideas and strategies that made it a reality. At the end of the year my final sales came in at $257,000. There were 7 people in the entire national sales force that reached that level of sales. I felt like I had learned and applied a great secret.

Affirmations

Napoleon Hill in his landmark book "Think and Grow Rich" revealed the incredible insight he gained about the subconscious mind and how it works,

Hill said, "Nature has so built man that he has absolute control over the material which reaches his subconscious mind, through his five senses." According to Hill the mind resembles "a fertile garden spot, in which weeds will grow in abundance, if the seeds of more desirable crops are not sown therein. Autosuggestion is the agency of control through which an individual may voluntarily feed his subconscious mind on thoughts of a creative nature, or, by neglect, permit thoughts of a destructive nature to find their way into this rich garden of the mind."

By following Hill's instructions of *persistent repetition* mixed with *strong emotion*, affirmations communicate the object of your desire directly to your subconscious mind in a spirit of absolute faith. Through repetition of this procedure, you voluntarily create thought habits which are favorable to your efforts to transmute desire into its (material) equivalent."

Autosuggestion is the term Hill used for what today is commonly referred to as the use of affirmations. Affirmations are statements used to program your subconscious mind. Don't forget what Napoleon Hill said - the strong positive emotions you feel when repeating your affirmations are important!

The more you feed your subconscious mind with positive messages and affirmations, the sooner it gets the message and starts to work in alignment with your goals. When you work with affirmations they need to be written and said in a positive language, and in the present tense. Commit to saying your chosen affirmations a minimum of three times a day: once in the morning when you first wake up, at mid-day, and again just before going to sleep. Preferrably repeat them as often as you can remember throughout the day, even as many as 50 times, for a period of 30 days. Of course the more you repeat them the sooner they will become a part of you.

I suggest you may want to write your affirmations on an Affirmations Card that you can carry around with you and easily refer to. Once you know them by heart, you won't need the card any longer. Or you can make an MP3 of them for you to listen to while you jog, walk, drive, or clean the house.

Here is a list of 12 tips for achieving success with affirmations:

1. Take action, start right away.

2. Be persistent and consistent

3. Use good emotions! Feel the feelings of having or reaching your goal.

4. Be specific about what you want.

5. Stay focused, choose two or three affirmations and use them for 30 days.

6. Write your affirmations on a small card and keep it with you at all times.

7. Write your affirmations in the present tense.

8. Use positive language in your affirmations.

9. Repeat your affirmations a minimum of three times a day.

10. Repeat your affirmations as many times as you remember throughout the day.

11. Put reminder notes around your house or office.

12. Make it fun.

The purpose of affirmations is to:

- Create an emotional state with a high vibrational frequency.

- Plant new beliefs in the subconscious mind.

- Keep in mind, the subconscious mind doesn't know the difference between something that is imagined and something that is real. It's possible that the emotional frequencies of an imagined event can be even more powerful than those of a real event.

Affirmations are most effective if they are:

1. Done in a meditative state.

2. Include visualization and emotion, words like, "I feel_____________," "I see_____________."

3. Stated in the present, as if the thing being affirmed is already accomplished: "I am _____________."

Here is an example: "**I feel** <u>thrilled</u> and <u>joyful</u> because **I see** my name on the New York best seller's list. I am now a bestselling author. This affirmation is emotional, it uses visualization, and it is stated in the present tense.

Re-framing

Reframing is the ability to see that God is working in everything for your good. It is the belief that the Universe in conspiring in your behalf. A successful reframer is a person who can be what Jack Canfield refers to as an "inverse paranoid," or someone who is obsessed with the belief that everything is conspiring for their good.

A boy went out in the backyard with his baseball bat and ball. As he threw the ball up into the air, he said to himself: "I'm the greatest hitter in the world" and as the ball came down he took a mighty swing and missed. "Strike one!" He said to himself. As he threw the ball up the second time, again he said to himself: "I'm the greatest hitter in the world," and as the ball came down he took another mighty swing and missed again. "Strike two!" As he threw the ball up the third time, again he said: "I'm the greatest hitter in the world," but as the ball came down he swung and missed, "Strike three!" For a moment a concerned look came over his face, then his eyes lit up and he shouted: "I'm the greatest pitcher in the world!" This is a perfect example of re-framing.

Ronald Reagan was a master re-framer. Once, when he was accused by his opponent of being too old to run for president, he reframed their accusation by saying: "Oh, that's just their youth and inexperience talking. We won't hold it against them." He had a natural ability to turn things around and put a new positive energy to them.

Emotions of fear, doubt, scarcity, resentment and unworthiness are ego based. These emotions are not only the cause of uneasiness), but they also keep us dissonant from the source of all goodness and blessing When we are connected with our Divine Source, there are no limitations, but to establish that connection we must reframe, or eliminate vibrational signals that are limited, or dissonant from Divine Purpose.

Reframing Questions

Have you ever noticed how different the world looks from the window of an airplane at 23,000 feet? The vantage point from which we see things has a great effect on what we believe, think and feel about things. If we are only seeing things from a vantage point of looking up at our huge pile of problems, we are seeing limited options, and we are going to feel discouraged. The language the Universe understands is the language of emotion. Emotions are the vibrational signal we send and that gets mirrored back into our lives. What if we could see our situation from 23,000 feet instead of from deep inside our pile of problems?

Exercise: On a piece of paper draw two circles, one on the left-hand side of the paper and one on the right-hand side. Then draw an arrow from the left-hand circle to the right-hand circle.

In the left-hand circle put the words, "Where I am now," and in the right-hand circle put the words, "Where I want to be." Under "Where I am now" list some of the conditions of your current situation. Under the words "Where I want to be" list the conditions you want to come into your life. Now you are looking at your situation from a much higher vantage point. With the help of a higher vantage point you are ready to ask yourself the reframing questions.

By using reframing questions we are doing two things: first, we are changing the emotions we are sending out to the Universe, and second, we are setting the filter of our Reticular Activating System to search the 40 million bits of information it receives from the Universe each second, and find the information we need to move from where we are now to where we want to be.

This much broader vantage point reframes our current beliefs giving us inspired feelings of hope and excitement that attract more of the same into our lives. Limiting beliefs can usually be reframed simply by asking the following questions:

- How can I?
- What if?

Reframing can also be done by filling in the blanks in the statements below:

- "Even though ____________, I am open to __________.
- "Even though____________, I choose to __________.

Here are some examples:

If I you are struggling with feelings of "unworthiness", you would begin by saying:

"**Even though** I am feeling unworthy, **how can I** see this differently?"

"**Even though** I am feeling unworthy, **what if** I could feel completely different?"

"**Even though** I feel unworthy, **I am open to** <u>the complete opposite being true</u>."

"**Even though** I feel unworthy, **I choose to** <u>unconditionally love and accept myself</u>."

Reframing is opening your subconscious to the complete opposite of whatever limiting belief you have accepted as truth. It is a very powerful tool, especially when combined with EFT or "tapping," which we will go into shortly.

By accepting the belief that your worthiness is a prerequisite for connecting to God, then the belief itself becomes a self-fulfilling prophecy, keeping you in a state of separation. Unless the belief is reframed, your emotions will remain dissonant from your source.

You can use the same process with the emotion of "fear."

"Even though I am feeling fear, what if I could feel completely different?"

"Even though I am feeling fear, how can I see this differently?"

"Even though I feel fear, I am open to <u>the complete opposite being true</u>."

"Even though I feel fear, I choose to <u>unconditionally love and accept myself</u>."

Paulo Coelho's book "The Alchemist" is a parable about the journey we all take, a journey where we learn that our only obligation is to realize our destiny (Divine Purpose). It is a parable about the faith, power, and courage we all have within us to pursue the intricate path of our own "personal legend."

It is a story of a boy who goes on a journey in search of his "personal legend" and he meets an Alchemist who becomes his spiritual mentor. At an important turning point in the story, the Alchemist teaches the boy this principle, "If a person is living out his personal legend, he knows everything he needs to know. There is only one thing that makes a dream impossible to achieve: the fear of failure." (Paulo Coelho, "The Alchemist," 141) And when we want something, all the universe conspires in helping us achieve it.

Other aspects of fear that you might consider reframing are:

- Fear of leaving comfort zones – (the unknown)

- Fear of failure – of loosing

- Fear of taking responsibility (increased responsibilities) – the expectations of others, facing the challenges of life, facing resistance, problems and stresses. (avoiding life)

- Fear of people's opinions

- Fear of rejection and disappointment

Other purposes of reframing could be:

- **To remove a mindset of doubt:** This allows you to move act on your Divine Purpose with the assurance that the way has already been provided. It is an inspired knowing that the resources, the people, the knowledge are coming.

- **To remove a mindset of scarcity:** When you are aligned with your divine purpose, limitations simply don't exist. You begin to think in terms of miracles. You experience an inner knowing that everything you need is on the way. There is no anxiety, fear, doubt or impossibility.

One of the main weaknesses of mankind is the average man's familiarity with the word impossible.

Meditation

"To a mind that is still, the whole Universe surrenders."

– Chang Tsu

> *"Meditation is an essential travel partner on your journey of personal transformation. Meditation connects you with your soul, and this connection gives you access to your intuition, your heartfelt desires, your integrity, and the inspiration to create a life you love."*
>
> - Sarah McLean

It is much easier to change the frequencies of our thoughts and emotions if they are not influenced by subconscious limiting beliefs. Meditation is the strongest means by which we can bridge the inner world and the outer world. Mediation is valuable because it helps slow down the activity of the brain caused by stress, anxiety and urgency. These emotions create a vibrational signal that is dissonant from spiritual connection. Slowing down brainwave acitivity is the most effective way to get past the gatekeeper.

The first step is to start "tuning in" to the energy of your Divine Source – that unseen energy that's within you and all around you. There is a spiritual side of you that needs to be reawakened and brought to the forefront of your awareness. And the best way to do that is by spending at least 10 minutes daily quieting your mind, relaxing your body, and focusing inward.

To understand the value of meditation we need to understand how the electrical vibrations in the brain effect what we resonate with. Learning how to consciously utilize your brainwave patterns enables you to experience greater resonance with the energy of your Divine Source.

There are four levels of consciousness that we are capable of experiencing: Beta, Alpha, Delta, and Theta.

With the help of modern technology these brainwave states are easily measurable. An EEG machine can tell us how many Hz per second our brains are creating, or the level of brain activity that we are operating at.

It is important to understand that the higher the Hz that our brains are creating, the more unfocused and chaotic our thought process becomes.

Do you seem to be unable to progress in a certain area of your life? Is there a level of success you can't seem to get past? Subconscious programming actually has more to do with your level of success than hard work, education, intelligence or even positive thinking.

If you've tried affirmations or reframing and only experienced limited results, it is because you are experiencing subconscious resistance. Resistance occurs when you have deep-seeded subconscious beliefs that override your conscious beliefs (the Elephant is refusing to be controlled by the rider).

To understand how this programming occurs, let's discuss the four levels of consciousness our brains can experience: They are Beta, Alpha, Delta, and Theta.

Beta - This is the "awake" state that most adults experience while conscious. Beta readings can vary between (14 Hz to over 100 Hz). The lower the Hz number, the more peace and calm we experience, while the higher the Hz number, the more we experience panic, fear, and anxiety.

Alpha - The Alpha state ranges from 8 Hz to 13.9 Hz and is known as a relaxation state, much like you would experience during meditation, going to sleep, and waking up out of sleep. This is when you are most in-tune with intuition, source, and spirit.

Theta - In Theta, the measurements range between 4 Hz and 7.9 Hz. This is the equivalent of a dreaming sleep state, or a deep meditative state. For infants, toddlers, and very young children, this is also known as "sponge mode." In this brainwave state their brains are encoding all the messages they receive from parents, teachers and care-givers. As they do this, they are rapidly forming beliefs about dangers, self-image, self-esteem, as well as, money and success. Theta waves are also conducive to visualization and creativity and the mind in this very relaxed state is even more receptive to suggestion and hypnosis. Here, too, our brain hemispheres are synchronized and we experience whole brain functioning.

Delta - And finally Delta which is below 4 Hz, which is synonymous with a dreamless sleep state or coma type state. Delta brainwaves are most prevalent during deep, dreamless sleep. The delta state is a mostly unconscious state that is essential to one's physical, emotional, psychological and spiritual wellbeing. People who are able to achieve a state of delta relaxation through meditation will sometimes describe spiritual encounters and out of body experiences. The delta state is perfect for inducing profound spiritual experiences, healing and deep subconscious re-patterning. Delta frequency brainwave entrainment music is also a fantastic cure for insomnia.

This is the brainwave state of babies in the womb. In this state they are already forming beliefs. Children are able to learn things so quickly because their brains are in a Theta wave dominant state. This is why it's so much easier to learn a language at a very young age.

Once we reach the age of 6 or 7 our brain switches to a Beta wave state, which is more of a conscious and awake state.

In Beta state your brain develops a filter between the conscious and subconscious minds. This filter prohibits new information from entering the subconscious mind.

When you are in a relaxed and serene state you enter more of an Alpha wave state. In the Alpha state it is easier for new thoughts and beliefs to pass through the filter. New beliefs can be formed if this is done with consistent repetition.

With very deep meditation you can access a Theta wave state. In Theta the filter between our conscious and subconscious minds is removed, making it possible for new information, like affirmations to pass into the subconscious mind and create new empowering beliefs that can reprogram your mind for success very quickly.

As adults there are two ways we can get past the filter and create new beliefs to reprogram our minds for success. First, we can sneak information past the conscious mind filter (gatekeeper) by combining meditationand affirmations at a Beta State, or we can remove the filter entirely by combining meditation, deep relaxation and affirmations at an even deeper Theta State.

Surrender to Greater Intelligence

*"You can't solve a problem using the same mind
that caused the problem in the first place."*
–Albert Einstein

Surrender means giving up the worry and stress of trying to fix your problems with that same mind that caused the problem. Surrender involves giving up trying to know all the answers with our conscious Beta mind and accepting there is a greater part of us that does. Our Theta mind is greater intelligence – it is unlimited. It has access to every piece of information in the Universe instantaneously.

Remember the Beta mind is for logical analyzing. It cannot comprehend the subconscious programming that is driving it.doesn't have a grasp for how to solve high end problems. We surrender by admitting that our Beta mind doesn't know the answers, but that there is a greater part of us that does. Our Theta mind is greater intelligence – it is unlimited. It has access to every piece of information in the Universe instantaneously.

Einstein is widely regarded as one of the greatest scientific minds of our time. He profoundly altered the way we look at ourselves and the universe. An article written by Craing Pearson MD shows that Eisnstein was a familiar with the teachings of Mahirishi Mahesh Yogi the founder of Transcendential meditation and that his teachings had a profound influence on him.[44]

In a letter Einstein wrote to Queen Elizabeth of Belgium (1876-1965) he is quoted as saying:

"Still there are moments when one feels free from one's own identification with human limitations and inadequacies. At such moments, one imagines that one stands on some spot of a small planet, gazing in amazement at the cold yet profoundly moving beauty of the eternal, the unfathomable: life and death flow into one, and there is neither evolution nor destiny; only being."[45])

Einstein also said: "The finest emotion of which we are capable is the mystic emotion. Herein lies the germ of all art and all true science. Anyone to whom this feeling is alien, who is no longer capable of wonderment and lives in a state of fear is a dead man. To know that what is impenetrable for us really exists and manifests itself as the highest wisdom and the most radiant beauty, whose gross forms alone are intelligible to our poor faculties — this knowledge, this feeling . . . that is the core of the true religious sentiment. In this sense, and in this sense alone, I rank myself among profoundly religious men."[46])

The "mystic emotion" Einstein refers to does not imply "mysterious" or "incomprehensible." The word *mystic* stems from Greek word meaning, simply, *to close*, i.e., the eyes. In the Transcendental Meditation technique we have a simple procedure for closing the eyes, diving within, and experiencing the field of pure consciousness, "the germ of all art and all true science," as Einstein worded it —— indeed, the germ of all creation.[47]

Einstein, one of the greatest scientific minds of our time understood and drew upon the "germ of all creation" – meditation and it is believed that it was in a Theta state that Einstein received the theory of relativity - E=mc2

Arthur Zajonic says that: " We think of <u>meditation</u> as following the breath, but for Einstein meditation was following thought." Einstein meditated while asking, "What would it be like to ride light?" "Einstein's analytic meditation led to his theory of relativity.

(⁸Understanding this helps our conscious mind relax and let go rather than feeling anxious and worried. Surrendering to our greater intelligence allows us to bring in knowledge and information, by commanding our subconscious while in a Theta state. This is how we reprogram our subconscious mind.

The only thing you have to do is release the "ego" of thinking your conscious mind has the answers. This is certainly a very different approach than what we've been taught about "just being positive" or "not allowing negative thoughts." It's impossible to just "be positive!" What we really need to do is embrace what we're thinking right now, and let our thinking reveal to us what we want to change.

Once a meditative state is reached, the subconscious mind can be given instructions. Your subconscious mind is far more powerful than any computer and it knows instantly what files to delete and which ones to rewrite. You do this by giving the subconscious mind suggestions or affirmations. Don't tell the subconscious "how" or "when" to do things, or how things should turn out. It is important to remain detached from the outcome completely. Just state your intention and let the subconscious do its work.

In a Theta brain-wave state you can speak directly to the subconscious mind. You can command it using a 3-part system.

1. "I don't know how I'm going to _______________________."
2. "I only know that I create _________________ right now!"
3. "I am fulfilled!"

This reprograms our subconscious beliefs, which changes the frequency of our emotions to resonate with those things we want to manifest in our lives. The Universe then provides the best way to make this happen which is in line with our Divine Purpose. Let go and let the subconscious do it's work.

By commanding your subconscious mind in a theta state you can also:

- Create a new reality. Benefit from a peaceful, calm, relaxed awareness of the possibility of a solution.

- Develop and raise your own intuition.

- Have vivid dreams and new information which will begin to arrive in your dream state.

- Become more connected to your true self and to other people.

- Learn to give up worry and stress. Worry and stress are the least effective method for accomplishing what you want. The reason we worry is because we believe that worrying will make us take action to solve something, or get a certain result.

Surrendering to your Theta mind state works so much faster than doing affirmations in a conscious Beta state. This is because the filter between your subconscious and conscious minds is inactive when you are in Theta. You can find Theta Binaural Beats Meditations on Youtube. Be sure you listen to them with stereo headphones on.

The principle of resonance is always in operation and is always attracting that which you are broadcasting through your emotions. If you understand how it operates you can learn to consciously create a vibrational state that attracts what you desire.

When your brain is having high, rapid electrical pulsations, it is actually operating at a much lower energy frequency than the universe operates at. In other words, the more anxious and fearful you are the more dramatically you reduce your bandwidth to the spiritual realm.

As physical brain function slows, it in essence opens the gateway to the spiritual realm and allows us to connect with spirit (Source Energy / Divine Intelligence), or whatever you choose to call it. That is why sleep is an escape from the anxiety experienced during waking hours, though it tends to return when you are awake, and the process that initiated the fear and anxiety begins again.

One of our biggest deterrents to Divine Purpose is the nonstop, overwhelming thoughts that relentlessly race through our heads as we attempt to juggle so many different pieces of life and usually end up finding ourselves unfulfilled at every turn. By re-activating anxious thoughts when we wake, brain wave activity increases, and the emotions of fear and anxiety are re-created.

As the brain's Hz is raised, we begin to emanate a lower vibrational frequency, making it impossible to focus our energies on the things we desire.

In other words if you are vibrating in fear, you are literally broadcasting a frequency of fear that in turn attracts energies that harmonize with fear. As a result you attract more of that which you don't want.

The principle of resonance isn't biased and doesn't make judgments concerning what is attracted to you. It only delivers precisely what you are asking for through the vibrational frequency you broadcast as your thoughts and emotions.

A good way to monitor the level of your mental activity is to observe the state of your physical body. A tense body is the sign of a tense mind. In order to continually stay in a vibrational frequency that attracts what is desired, it is necessary to maintain the lowest energy activity from within the brain as possible.

This is best accomplished through meditation, which slows brain activity, and brings a sense of peace, calm, well-being and inner-knowing.

With meditation you can "consciously" utilize the principle of resonance, to attract Divine Purpose. Unfocused and chaotic brain waves keep you dissonant from Divine Purpose.

Brainwave entrainment

> *"For every deep rooted belief and habit you have, your brain forms evidence, opinions and behaviors that support your belief and habit . . . even if it's not what you really want in your life."*
>
> – John Assaraf

Brainwave entrainment is a somewhat new technology that is engineered to bring your mind into a specific level of Theta which is specifically designed to help you to re-organize your brain to a higher level.

It can be used to interrupt the loop of your current neuro-chemistry with the use of tones, or sound frequencies. These frequencies have a physiological effect that trains your neural pathways to relieve stress and anxiety. Using brainwave technology gets you back to your natural state by interrupting the pattern of looking for potential "danger." This allows you to see solutions and opportunities that you cannot see when you are focused on problems.

EFT or Meridian Tapping

To understand how EFT works it is essential to understand that everything is energy and every obstacle in our lives is at some point a disruption in the energy system of our body, mind and spirit. The obstacles that we face in life are the result of resistance, at an energy level that needs to be cleared out.

A lot of people who've learned about the "Law of Attraction" have adopted the belief that they have to keep themselves from having any negative thoughts or feelings – that is impossible, it's not the way we are created to function.

It's not about never having negative thoughts or feelings; it's about the body, mind and spirit processing them and releasing them. We all have painful emotions that get repressed and our body, mind and spirit need to process them and release them.

Emotional Freedom Techniques (EFT) is a technique that not only releases negative emotional resistance, but it can also reframe negative thoughts, and embed new beliefs. EFT, also known as "Tapping," is a cutting-edge technique that , in my experience, is a powerful tool for transforming the energy signal of your beliefs, thoughts and emotions, making it easier than ever before to experience resonance.

Dr. Joe Vitale, who is well known for his part in the movie "the Secret," says that he has been using EFT himself for over 20 years when he is having feelings of "being stuck," indecision, anxiety, or any emotion that's in the way of feeling peace in the moment. He uses EFT anytime his emotional energy is keeping him from being all he can be. He says it is one of the most powerful techniques he has ever used and he continues to use it on a regular basis.

The concept is that you are tapping with your fingers on meridian points in the body while repeating certain statements. For instance, if you were going to give a speech and you were feeling anxious about it you could begin tapping while repeating words like "Even though I'm feeling anxious about giving this speech I choose to release the anxiety and feel completely at ease and confident."

What we're learning is that there are meridian points throughout the body where negative emotions can get stuck. Tapping sends an electrical signal through the meridians clearing out the negative emotion. It's something that, until you experience it, sounds a little strange.

Affirmations can be effective for creating high-frequency emotional states, however, if you've used affirmations and found yourself saying: "yea, affirmations are nice, if only I could really believe it."

When our conscious   affirmations aren't tapping into the

subconscious mind in a way that creates a new belief, EFT or Tapping can be very effective. Tapping implants the affirmation into your belief system (the subconscious). Tapping not only helps reframes take hold, it helps you create them.[40] The concept of tapping may seem a little weird at first; I know it did to me. But I was open to giving it a try because I was sick of living a dissonant life. I was completely ready to experience a powerful connection to my Divine Purpose.

Over the years I have found affirmations, visualization and reframing to be effective, but when I began combining them with tapping an amazing transformation occurred.

My wife will attest to the fact that within a few weeks of beginning EFT, a transformation was taking place. I was much happier, more optimistic and fun-loving. Before I began tapping I would wake up depressed and overwhelmed, but after a few weeks I began waking up with an excited optimism about the day. My anxiety and limiting beliefs seemed to be fading.

Before I began tapping I worried constantly about money, but within a few weeks I began experiencing a connection to the energy of abundance.

So what is tapping? We could say its "psychological acupuncture." It works in a way that is similar to acupuncture, just without the needles. For thousands of years, Eastern medicine practitioners have believed that our bodies contain energy pathways called "meridians". These energy pathways often become blocked or sluggish due to trauma, illness, and negative thought patterns.

When acupuncture needles are inserted into the skin at certain points along these meridians, it releases energy that may be "stuck" and allows the free flow of energy through the meridians again. When the stuck energy is released, it usually clears up the problem(s) that were caused by the blockage. With EFT, you tap lightly on the meridian end points while tuning into the problem mentally and emotionally, and this releases the stuck energy.

Tapping is still fairly young compared to other alternative treatments, but it is quickly gaining in popularity and people are getting astounding results from it. It's being used successfully on mental, physical and emotional problems like addictions, post-traumatic stress, physical illnesses of almost every description, fears, phobias, weight problems, and even for _dissonance_ from your Divine Purpose.

After just a few minutes of tapping on a limiting belief, you'll notice that focusing on that belief no longer stirs up heavy emotions. (If it does, you may need to do several rounds of tapping to be sure you've cleared all of that negative energy.)

But that's not the end of the process when it comes to limiting beliefs. Next you'll need to replace that old, limiting belief with a better belief. Most of the time, that means focusing on a belief that is completely opposite of the original belief.

How EFT works

EFT is a technique that assists you in releasing "resistance." Resistance is what keeps us from allowing and receiving all the flow of Divine Energy.

When you have symptoms such as anxiety, pain or a block to success it means that you have blocked energy in your system. So with tapping you can unblock the energy and the symptom goes away.

Many times the reason the Law of Attraction doesn't give you what you want is because you have some type of an energy block. Remember, when you have a thought, a feeling or a fear that is a vibration, it is actually a frequency. What we do with tapping is target the block, release it and then the Law of Attraction has a very clear signal. It can now pick up your frequency more clearly and respond to it.

Think of an experience that made you angry or upset. If you continue to think about it, even if you try to ignore it, you're building more and more neural pathways of stress and upset. The fact that this process gets stronger over time makes it even more essential that we interrupt the process of creating these negatively based neural connections, because negative emotions and limiting beliefs get worse over time, not better.

Tapping interrupts this process. Tapping sends signal to the brain to react with calm, not with fear or upset. It has been proven to drastically reduce cortisol levels. This in turn reduces stress. Any time you think about something upsetting, whether it is an action that you're about to take or a disturbing memory, tapping helps to neutralize it.[50]

When you release *dissonant* emotional energy from your body, you improve your vibrational signal! When your vibrational signal improves, you *resonate* with Divine power and attract more of it into your life. So, when you tap to clear negative dissonant energies, what youare really doing is tapping to clear feelings of anger, frustration, resentment, jealousy, fear, anxiety, and anything else that is blocking your ability to resonate with your Divine Purpose.

You can learn the official version of EFT and download a Quick Start PDF guide at this website: http://www.eftuniverse.com

The Tapping Points

The points to tap on are pretty easy to learn, and once you've gone through a few rounds of tapping, they are easy to remember.

- The first point is located on the outside edge of either hand, about midway between the knuckle of your small finger and the base of your wrist. It's called the "Karate Chop Point" (because that's the part of the hand that would be used for a karate chop).

- Next is the point on the inner end of each eyebrow right on the edge of the eye socket. This is called the "Eyebrow Point."

- Next is the "Side of Eye" point, and it is on the outer side of each eye; once again right on the edge of the eye socket – not too close to the eyeball, and not too far back toward the temple – it's right on the outer bony edge of the eye socket.
- Next is the "Under the Eye" point, and once again it is right on the bony ridge of the eye socket, directly under the center of the eye.
- Next is the "Under the Nose" point, which is directly under the nose midway between the base of the nose and upper lip.
- Below that is the "Chin" point, also sometimes referred to as the "Under the Mouth" point. It's right in the crease between the lower lip and chin.
- Next is the "Collarbone" point, which is found approximately one inch below and one inch to either side of the "U" shaped notch where the collarbones meet.
- The "Under the Arm" point is located about four inches below the armpit on either side of the body, right about where a bra strap is for women, and roughly in line with the nipple for men.*
- Finally, the "Top of the Head" point is directly in the center of the crown of the head.

Don't worry too much about getting these points exactly right because as you tap the general area, vibrations will travel through the surrounding tissue and stimulate the point. Just being close to it is usually good enough to get results.

Here's how to use tapping to clear negative feelings and beliefs:

First try to get an idea of how strong the negative feelings are by rating them on a scale of 0-10 (10 being the strongest). Then jot that number down.

Then start tapping on the Karate Chop point, on the side of the hand, while stating the problem, as well as a positive intention. The Karate Chop point is a great point to start with because it helps clear any psychological resistance you may have to the tapping, or to the statements you'll be saying while you tap.

Example: "Even though I feel really frustrated about (state the problem), I deeply and completely accept myself anyway." It's always good to start out saying you deeply and profoundly accept yourself, because it helps to drop all resistance.

Then you move to the basic sequence of acupuncture points and you tap on them. For example, if youare right-handed, you would tap with two fingers of your right hand. As you do this you "state the problem." Essentially, what you are doing is "bringing up the document" in your brain so you can edit it. Think of it as a document on your computer. You need to call the vibration up, so you can reduce it and get it out of your system. So you need to focus on the problem while you are tapping.

If we are working on the problem of anxiety, our "set-up statement" would be: "Even though I have this anxiety I deeply and completely accept myself." Do this three times while tapping on the Karate-chop point. Then begin tapping through the following sequence:

- Eyebrow point – name the problem (this anxiety)
- Side of the eye – name the problem again
- Bottom of the eye –name the problem
- Under the nose – name the problem
- Chin point – name the problem
- Collar bone point- name the problem
- Under your arm pit four inches below - name the problem
- Top of the head - name the problem and say "I'm ready to let it go."

Now you have finished one round. So measure again on a scale from 1-10 where your anxiety is.

***

Repeat the same or a similar statement three times while tapping continuously on the side of the hand.

Then start tapping on any or all of the points. You can go through all of the points, or you can focus on just one or two – let your intuition guide you.

As you tap the points continuously, focus on the problem or feeling you want to clear, really tuning into those heavy, negative feelings. Say a few words that help you express it.

Example: "This frustration…; I'm so tired of these _________ problems; I'm sick of _________; I get so angry sometimes…; I feel terrible…; I get so sick and tired…; I need to clear whatever is blocking success in my life; it's so heavy and unpleasant . . ."

Usually after just a few minutes of tapping while focusing on the negative feelings, you will feel a noticeable improvement. Gauge the intensity of your feelings again, and if they are reduced but still not at a zero, do a few more minutes of tapping and speaking aloud whatever is bothering you.

Then start tapping in a few positive statements like, "I'm ready to let go of this frustration; it doesn't serve me; it does me no good; all it does is drag me down." Essentially what this technique allows you to do is tap into Universal energy.

Here is another example. This time we'll deal with the specific emotion of anxiety.

<u>Ask yourself</u>: "What am I anxious about?

"I feel anxious about facing the details of a new day."

<u>Ask yourself</u>: "What is the belief I'm holding on to?

It's the belief that "today is going to be painful and stressful. I just have to man up and deal with it." (Like diving into freezing water)

Ask yourself: "on a scale of 1 to 10 how painful is this negative emotion?

If it is 7 or higher, begin a round of tapping while repeating the phrase: "I feel very anxious about the details of my day." After you've gone through all the tapping points, ask yourself again: "on a scale of 1 to 10 how painful is this negative emotion? If it is less than a 7, begin another round of tapping, this time repeating the phrase: "Even though I feel very anxious about the details of my day _______________________ . Fill in the blank with the options below.

- **I am open to** feeling joyful and optimistic about all the details of the day
- **I am open to** those feelings disappearing
- **What if I** could hardly wait to dive in?
- **What if I** could be totally excited?
- **How can I** feel peaceful and calm?

Then tap another round while repeating the phrase: "Even though I feel very anxious about the details of my day _______________________ . Again, fill in the blank with the options below.

- **I choose to** see the new day with extreme passion and excitement
- **I choose to** give off and connect to an amazing vibrational frequency!
- **I choose to** be a completely new person!
- **I choose to** be enabled by divine power!
- **I choose** a power greater that myself.

By now your level of anxiety should be greatly reduced and you will also find that you're feeling inspired and radiating at a much higher, more positive frequency.

Tapping can also help reshape your neural pathways. Our neural pathways get shaped by what we habitually focus on. Tapping enables us to begin changing our focus and reframing our thinking to a higher energy, more inspired pattern of thought.

Love and Gratitude

We have already discussed that there are essentially two emotions:

love and fear, and that all others stem from them. Love is at the top of the scale of emotions that resonate with spirit and Divine Purpose and fear is at the bottom of emotions that are dissonant.

Love and gratitude are at the heart of Divine Purpose. They are the highest, most powerful emotions and the key to Universal energy, or Source Energy. The way you feel about any given subject is the most important thing when it comes to manifesting Divine Purpose.

Gratitude is a powerful manifestation tool because it dramatically changes your feelings about whatever youare focusing on. And by changing your feelings, youare changing your vibrational signal.

Your vibrational signal is a command to the universe. Because gratitude is one of the highest, purest emotions you can feel, you are commanding the universe to send you more of whatever you happen to be focused on emotionally, positive or negative. Gratitude is so powerful because it immediately moves you spiritually, into a s high vibrational state, a state that resonates with your divine purpose.

When you say "thank you" for something – even if you don't yet have it – you are resonating with the vibrational signal of that which you desire. Universal Energy, by means of universal laws, sends more of it to you. Practicing gratitude for the things you desire actually brings more of them into your life.

It may not manifest instantly, but it doesn't take long for this principle to work if you are consistent in your feelings. Keep the vibrational signal strong!

Consistency is the key! Be consistent and constant with your focus on gratitude. If you only do it once a week, or once a month, you won't see much progress. Focus on it daily, focus on it many times a day for a few minutes, and youwill see amazing results.

If you combine your feelings of gratitude with the techniques we've been discussing (meditation, affirmations, reframing, tapping and visualization) your vibrational signal will be strong and powerful.

Practicing the emotions of love and gratitude are two additional ways to renew the mind. Truly understanding the power of gratitude can change your life forever!

Because our emotions are somewhat like the weather in the way they change from day to day, I think this poem, titled by B.J. Gallagher gives us great insight on how to reframe them in a positive way:

Do you want to learn how to immediately raise your energetic vibration so you can instantly attract positive people and opportunities into your life? It's the act of expressing gratitude for the things that you're happy to have in your life. I suggest keeping a Love and Gratitude Journal and at the end of the day write down all the things from that day that you loved and were grateful for.

A blind boy sat on the steps of a building with a hat by his feet. He held up a sign which said: 'I am blind, please help.' There were only a few coins in the hat.

A man was walking by. He took a few coins from his pocket and dropped them into the hat. He then took the sign, turned it around, and wrote some words. He put the sign back so that everyone who walked by would see the new words.

Soon the hat began to fill up. A lot more people were giving money to the blind boy. That afternoon the man who had changed the sign came to see how things were. The boy recognized his footsteps and asked, "Were you the one who changed my sign this morning? What did you write? "

The man said, "I only wrote the truth. I said what you said but in a different way."

I wrote: ' Today is a beautiful day but I cannot see it.'

Both signs told people that the boy was blind. But the first sign simply said the boy was blind. The second sign told people that they were so lucky that they were not blind. Should we be surprised that the second sign was more effective?

Be thankful for what you have.[51]

***

Until you have gone without something, it is easy to forget to be grateful. So practice gratitude for the things you normally take for granted like your health and the love of those around you

The ability to love yourself is the first step in transforming your energy signal. The inability to love your "self" sets up a cycle of shame and self-abandonment which in turn leads to anxiety, depression, addiction, aloneness, and relationship failure. A recovered connection to Divine Purpose necessitates an ability to love your "self" rather than abandon your "self." It necessitates a consistent connection with your personal source of spiritual guidance. Any type of emotional disease is rooted in a separation of self from source. We are not whole if we have separated ourselves from love of self, love of God and love of others.

Spiritual wholeness is also measured by the way you treat other people. It is measured by the love you allow to operate through you. First Corinthians 13 tells us about the characteristics of love. One characteristic is that it is not rude. That means, when we are walking in love, we treat other people with courtesy and respect. Are you courteous to other people? Are you kind to the person at the checkout counter that may be moving too slowly for you? Are you gentle when you are driving down the highway and someone cuts you off? Are you patient with your family and coworkers? These are all ways we show love. These are ways we connect vibrationally to Source Energy.

Scripture also tells us that love is patient. It is kind. It does not envy; it is not proud. It is not rude. Love is not easily angered, and it keeps no record of wrongs. Love never fails. In order to practice these characteristics we may have to choose to go above what we are feeling in the moment. That's because love is a choice. You can choose to walk in love toward people even when you don't feel like it. But when we do so, the energy of our feelings begins to transform. Through our agency we can transform our energy to align with Source Energy. Love is a critically important principle of Divine Purpose!

Love looks for ways to improve someone else's life. Love brings out the best in other people. Don't just get up in the morning thinking about yourself or how you can make your own life better. Think about how you can make someone else's life better. Ask yourself, "Who can I encourage today?" "Who can I build up?" You have something to offer those around you that no one else can give. Someone in your life needs your encouragement. Someone in your life needs to know that you believe in them. I believe God will hold us be responsible for the people He's put in our lives. He's counting on us to bring out the best in our family and friends.

Whenever we feel love or gratitude for anyone or anything, there is no humanness going on. It is Divine love. All of these techniques we've discussed in this chapter, all of the affirmations, all of the visualizations and emotional releasing techniques are for one reason, to lead us to a state of positivity so that we can then do what we are really here to do, which is to fulfill our Divine Purpose.

Exercise: Ask yourself:
- What am I focusing on?
- What am I not seeing?
- What is my subconscious mind resisting?
- What beliefs are keeping me limited?
- What is my frequency?

Summary

How do I apply this principle?

- Utilize the technique of affirmation
- Utilize the technique of reframing
- Utilize the technique of meditation

- Utilize the technique of EFT
- Seek to maintain a state of love and gratitude
- Benefits
- Experience greater freedom form mental dissonance
- Experience greater freedom from limiting beliefs
- Gain a greater ability to choose new beliefs, thoughts and emotions
- Gain a greater bandwidth to Source Energy
- Consequences
- Remain in mental dissonance
- Retain your limiting beliefs
- Retain a limited bandwidth to True Success
- Go to website at www.PrinciplesofDivinePurpose.com to access information on EFT
- Go to website at www.PrinciplesofDivinePurpose.com to access information on affirmations
- Go to my website at www.PrinciplesofDivinePurpose.com for a video on EFT/tapping and link to "Tapping into Ultimate Success."

Practice meditation

- Practice affirmations
- Practice reframing
- Practice Tapping
- Practice Gratitude
- Practice Love

CHAPTER FIVE

How to Raise Your Frequency through Visualization!
Principle 5: Imagination

"Imagination is everything. It is the preview of life's coming events."

\- Albert Einstein

It is important to understand mind renewal techniques, because now as we move into visualization techniques a lot of your subconscious issues will come up. We use techniques such as EFT and affirmations for changing the vibrational frequency of our emotional state, where visualization actually changes our belief system. The subconscious mind doesn't recognize the difference between an image we create and reality.

The power of imagination

> *"When the imagination and will power are in conflict, are antagonistic, it is always the imagination which wins, without any exception."*
>
> – Emile Coue

Another way that we increase our bandwidth to Divine Intelligence is through the power of imagination. Remember, the subconscious mind is emotional and processes ideas simultaneously, using pictures.

Often we think of imagination as something that kids do, but we are all using the power of imagination all the time. Unfortunately, a lot of us learn to use it to create images of fear and doubt about our futures. Anxiety and worry are merely imagination habits used in a way that creates low-frequency vibrations.

What we are really doing when we're imagining, is exercising one of the most powerful mental faculties we've been given. When we play out scenarios in our imagination we have the chance to root-out and eliminate any conflicting vibrations. Visualization can be a very effective tool to help you work through resistance.

Imagination starts the process of creation, so it is important that we use this power to create a future aligned with our dreams and passions and not a future aligned with our fears and doubts. Here's an example of the power of positive imagination:

Story of the Coach's Helper

Not long ago I saw a news story about an autistic boy who was the coach's helper for his high school's basketball team. He mostly did little things like bringing water and handing out towels. As he was attending to his duties, he would imagine himself playing for the team. He was always rehearsing in his mind the incredible things he would do in game situations.

His passion and devotion to the team earned him so much respect from the coach that in the final game of the season the coach allowed him to suit up for the game. Then with four minutes left in the game, the coach unexpectedly substituted him in.

His first shot was a twenty-footer from the right baseline that missed everything. His second was about the same, but on his third shot he drained a three-pointer, and something just clicked. The images he had rehearsed took over, and he began to hit shot after shot. He made six straight shots, mostly three pointers, for a total of twenty points. With each succeeding shot the crowd grew wilder and wilder. When he hit his final three-pointer as time was running out, the scene became utter mayhem. Because of his autism, he was used to feeling different, but this was very different from his real life experience This was something he had only experienced in his imagination!

An "outside-in" focus could never have brought this type of result. His success was the result of the images he had played over every day in his mind - like a movie. Without the principle of imagination, this situation would have been considered a fluke. But this was no fluke! The script of this movie had been written and rehearsed many times before it actually played out. This is the amazing creative power God has placed within each of us![52]

Preview Your New Image

"All things are created twice. There's a mental or
first creation, and a physical or second creation
to all things"

- Stephen Covey

"Creative Imagination" is the process by which the finite mind has direct communication with infinite intelligence. It is the faculty through which "hunches" and "inspirations" are received. It is by this faculty that basic or new ideas are handed over to man.

It is through this faculty that thought vibrations from the minds of others are received."[53]

True Success begins as an image in the mind

Human beings have been endowed with powerful God-given creative faculties, and the act of creation begins as we create a vision or an image in our mind. Imagination is the mental faculty out of which visions arise.

Everything that has ever been created started out as an image in somebody's mind, like watching a movie. One of our biggest problems is that we don't comprehend the power of our own minds. Creative thought is energy in motion, and when you put your movie into your mind it begins to move into form.

Preview your New Life

"Imagination is the beginning of creation. You
imagine what you desire, you will what you
imagine and at last you create what you will."

- George Bernard Shaw

Visualization

Visualization is basically the process of imagining yourself having achieved your ideal life, down to the smallest details. Visualization is the most effective way to achieve an abundant vibration.

John Assaraf, an expert in the science of visualization, tells a story of moving into his new beautiful dream home in California and as he was unpacking boxes he came across a vision board that he had created years before. To his amazement, on that vision board, was a picture of the home he had just moved into. Not a picture of a similar home, but a picture of the very home he had just purchased. These were pictures he had cut out of Dream Homes Magazine a few years before. He had never been to the home, he had just imagined himself owning the home one day. The power of his imagination actually manifested the exact same home in his life.

He has never said "I will one day live in that exact same home." He just felt the excitement of imagining he would one day own a home just like that.

When I was first introduced to this concept I heard about the idea of making a vision board. A vision board is simply a collection of pictures or images that represent the dreams and passions you want to manifest in your life. I later heard about the idea of mind movies, Which is creating your own video depicting the images of things you want to manifest combined with inspirational music. As I began practicing this principle, the first thing I did was go to Google and search for beautiful images that represented the things I wanted to manifest in my life. Next, I pasted them on a word document. Thirdly, I typed my affirmations under the pictures that matched up with that set of affirmations. Lastly, I found inspirational music that elicited deep emotional feelings as I visualized my new life.

We all run movies in our minds, and our emotions are the result of the part we are playing in those movies. If you are worried, it's because you are imagining the problems and failures you have created in your mental movie. To fully experience True Success you need to imagine yourself already living the life you want to lead. You need to feel the life as if it were true right now. Begin re-scripting your mental movies and create a better future!

To visualize effectively it is important that you are emotionally connected to your outcome. Without the emotional connection you just won't get the same results. Emotion is one of the most powerful ways to change your thought patterns. You cannot change your vibrational signal without experiencing the emotion of that frequency.

Make visualization a full-body experience! What do you see, smell, taste, feel and hear? Get all of your senses involved. Use your capacity to pretend the way you did as child.

You can't be visualizing something vague that doesn't stir up any emotion, that's why you must be clear on what you want.

Like the autistic boy, you too, can create True Success in your imagination, and it will play out in ways that fulfill your dreams and passions. Remember, the more crystal-clear your images and emotions are, the more powerful your results will be. Here are some steps that might help:

Assignment

Create your own vision board or mind movies. Be sure to use pictures and music that cause a deep emotional response. Remember, emotion is the language the Universe understands and our subconscious minds don't know the difference between something imagined and something real.

If you will visualize regularly and keep a look out for the people and opportunities to help you achieve your affirmations, you will be shocked at how many things start falling into place for you all on their own. This is "the flow" of True Success.

Through the power of imagination you are planting in your subconscious the seeds of True Success. If you plant a carrot seed in the ground and nourish it with water and sunlight, it's going to grow. It's the same way with your mental movies. If you'll plant the seed of imagination and nourish it with emotion, your mental movies will begin to resonate with your dreams and they will bring forth the reality you've imagined.

Practicing this principle will put you in a select group of people. The average individual is not writing his own movies, he is only an extra in the wrong movie. As long as you can't imagine what you want to create, it's not going to happen. If you can see it, it can come to pass. You have to envision good things happening before they ever will. And you can use visualization to continuallyimprove on the results you are currently getting.

If you want to connect to all the blessings and favor of your Divine Purpose, you need to enlarge your vision. You must conceive it in your mind and heart before you will receive it. This will never happen if you are entertaining negative, defeated and limiting thoughts. What you keep before your eyes will affect you. You will produce what you are continually seeing in your mind. If you see victory, success, health, abundance, joy, peace and happiness, your beliefs will begin to align with your vision, and those things will begin to manifest in your life.

Your Divine Purpose manifests in your life as you make room for abundance and increase in your thinking. Universal laws are designed to keep us increasing and reaching new heights. This universe operates by laws that are designed to support us in our desires to create and expand. Our agency is our power to choose the life we will create. The key word here is "create." And all things are created spiritually (mentally) before they manifest physically. This is where the role of our creative imagination comes into play.

If you don't think you can create an abundant life, it is not because the universe lacks the resources. The barrier is in your mind.

Be a Visionary

> *"Imagination is more important than knowledge. For knowledge is limited to all we now know and understand, while imagination embraces the entire world, and all there ever will be to know and understand."*
>
> –Albert Einstein

In the business world, we see people like Bill Gates, Steve Jobs and Walt Disney who were very successful because of their ability to be visionaries. True success in any endeavor is always created in the mind first.

Two things happen when we visualize:

1. Inwardly we are opening up the creativity of the subconscious mind. That is why when we combine affirmations with visualization we are creating a very powerful tool. Closing our eyes and seeing it as if it has already happened.

2. By adding the power of emotion, we give a command to our subconscious mind to figure out how to make this image a reality.

"Visualization" affects our beliefs, thoughts and emotions in ways that create powerful resonance with our Divine Purpose. Remember, the subconscious mind doesn't know the difference between something that is real and something that is imagined. Visualization puts us more powerfully in the feeling of what our mind is creating.

The whole idea behind visualization is how it affects our feelings. Just having an image in our mind will have no effect. Remember, it's our feelings that create our frequency. Our visualization needs to create powerful feelings of excitement, inspiration and passion. We need to use visualization to emotionally experience what we will feel when the thing we want is already part of our reality.

Visualization x Emotion x Repetition

"Vision is the art of seeing what is invisible to others."

- Jonathan Swift

We are constantly shaping our own brain chemistry without even realizing it. When we visualize something repeatedly with strong emotion, the repetition of that emotion begins to create new neural pathways. The strong emotions we associate with the image actually ingrains the image into our brains. The repetition causes our brain cells or neurons to fire over and over again. That's a scientific way of saying that the more we do something, the easier it is for us to do. And the easier it is for us to do, the more our brains will do it, because the brain becomes conditioned to the emotion of the repetition. This is the reason why we are drawn in any direction, positive or negative.

The Universe that God has created is run by infinite intelligence! Our planet is moving around the sun, the sun is in its orbit around black holes. There are Protons, Electrons and Quarks all working in perfect order and harmony. The intelligence of the Universe responds, not to our thinking, not to our words, but to our emotions, so if I am feeling and acting as if my dreams and passions are already mine, the Universe will match and mirror my emotions.

Everything we see manifested in our lives is a reflection of what's happening in the brain. Our brains do a couple of major things, first, they keep us alive and secondly, they make sure our outside world is an absolute mirror image of our internal world.

To use the analogy of a movie again, if we don't like what we're seeing on the movie screen, there is no reason to destroy the screen – instead we should change the reel. What's on the screen is only a reflection of what is being projected from the reel. Similarly, what is showing up in our lives is only a reflection of what is being projected from our minds. Our physical world always matches up with our internal world.

As soon as you can get the image in your mind to match what you want in your outside world, that is when you begin to attract the right people, the right mentors and teachers, the right books and cd's, the right opportunities. But mostly that is when you start to behave differently.[54]

Visualization Techniques

<u>Vision boards</u> – putting up pictures of the things you want that will conjure up the emotions of the things you want to manifest. If a vision board does nothing to create those powerful emotions them it is useless and if you are not using releasing techniques as you do it, it is useless as well. If you're not releasing those negative energies as they come up, you are just attracting more of that.

<u>Mind movies</u> –

- Engages multiple senses – audio, video.
- Taps into your sense of creativity.
- Fun and easy to create and change. It's okay to make changes as you identify things you thought you wanted, but begin to realize have nothing to do with who you are.

When Joel Osteen took over as Pastor for the Lakewood Church, after the passing of his father, he admitted that he had a very hard time seeing himself doing it. He felt overwhelmed and inadequate. He said that he had to play new recordings in his mind. The old recording said: "you're scared to death, you're going to forget what you're going to say, people aren't going to like you . . ."

For many years he had no desire to be a preacher, maybe because it wasn't the right time yet. But when his father died there was a new desire on the inside. He just knew he was supposed to step up and

Pastor the church. In his book "Living Your Best Life" He talks about listening to the "Still-small voice" telling him what he was supposed to do.

He said he believes God puts dreams and desires in our hearts. That's why he feels so passionate about telling people to follow their dreams. "If you have a desire in there I believe God has equipped you with what you need to fulfill it."

"I feel like this is what I was born to do. And I don't feel like its work, it's fun, I enjoy it doing it. I'm not saying it's not hard and it doesn't take work, but I enjoy doing it so I think that's where the sense of purpose and destiny comes of doing what you know you are supposed to do. And it's not work and it's not a burden.

He started talking to himself differently. He calls it "being positive toward yourself." He says there are a lot of people trying to fulfill their callings or their destinies but they have the wrong recordings playing inside. He calls it "fighting the good fight of faith."

He said: "You have to step out on faith and God gives you a little bit. He doesn't always give you the whole way." He talked about needing to raise $100 million to buy the Compaq Center and being either bold enough or dumb enough to give it a try and everything just fell into place.

"You just have to take a step of faith, and if you feel good about it in here . . . We only live once so we need to step out and live what God has put in our heart."

So when he first felt the impression to purchase the Compaq Center (previous home of the Houston Rockets) for the Lakewood Church, he said his initial thoughts were "how could this be? How could we ever get that facility? It's going to be too expensive. The city will never let a church use that. It's much too prominent." But he chose to expand his vision and let the seed take root. He said: "I conceived it on the inside. I began to "see" our congregation worshiping God in the Compaq Center in the heart of Houston."

Over the next few months, plenty of people told him, "It's never going to happen. You don't have a chance. You're wasting your time."[55] But it didn't matter. The seed was growing on the inside. At times it looked impossible, and they faced all kinds of challenges, but three and a half years later they came out victorious.

Connecting with our passion and purpose means visualizing what we want to achieve. As we visualize it over and over, what previously seemed impossible will begin to seem possible.

"Allow yourself to dream. And dream big dreams! Extraordinary people visualize not what's possible or probable, but the improbable and even the impossible. By visualizing them, they begin to make them possible."[56]

"We are limited, not by our abilities, but by our vision."

Where there is no vision, the people perish . . . (Proverbs 29:18)

See your new Image

I don't think there could be a better definition of True Success than this one by Deepak Chopra:

> *"Success is the expansion of happiness. It's forward progression in your life through the unfolding of your own vision."*
>
> – Deepak Chopra

I love sports, especially college football. The college team that I cheer for has only had three losing seasons in the last 30 years, and those three years were extremely painful for the program and the fans. Finally a new coach was brought in that had a new vision for the direction of the football program.

One of the first things the new coach did was to take the players on a trip up into the mountains where they built a big bonfire. He then had the players write down on big sheets of paper, all the reasons why they could not see the team succeeding. Then after they had presented all of their reasons, he had them take the lists they had created and cast them into the fire.

The next week he took all the players to the stadium and had them lie down on the field. He then asked the players to close their eyes and visualize as highlights of past championship seasons were piped in over the loud speakers.

Because the coach had a compelling vision, he was able to give his players a "new image" of themselves and the program. The team has never had a losing season since.

How do you see yourself? Do you see yourself as successful, healthy, upbeat and happy? Or do you say to yourself, "I'll never make it in life, my dreams will never come to pass?"

Stop for a minute and visualize in your mind a portrait of yourself. See in your countenance all the challenges and victories of your life. See in your features the weaknesses and   strengths you've inherited. See your successes and failures. See who you've become through your life's experiences.

Now imagine your life's portrait framed, and placed in a prominent place in your home. As you look at the portrait you've created, how do you feel? Remember your feelings are the signal you send out to the Universe. How do you see the events of your past? How do you see your mistakes? How do you see your weaknesses? How do you see your life's work? How do you see your adversities? And most importantly, how do you see your future?

Now, grab the canvas on which you've painted your own likeness, rip it from the frame, tear it up and throw it into the fire!

See His image of you

"The image God wants you to have of yourself has been distorted; the mirrors in which you have seen yourself . . . have been grossly cracked, delivering a contorted and distorted image of yourself. When you accept that warped image, you open yourself to depression, poverty or worse. If you are not careful you will begin thinking that the image you see in those cracked mirrors is a true reflection of the way life is supposed to be."[57]

Now ask God to show you His portrait of you, His image of your value and purpose. How would he paint you? Would he paint your weaknesses and failings or would He paint you according to your Divine Purpose and the True Success He created you to experience? His image of you would inspire you to live your Divine Purpose.

His portrait of you would obviously be different than the one you painted of yourself. So get rid of the self-image you have created for yourself. Come to know the image that God has of you.

See your Divine Worth

When I began my career as a personal coach, I was fortunate to have a great mentor. My father-in-law was not only a great mentor and an amazing personal coach, but he is also a deeply spiritual man. From time to time he worked with clients who struggled with their sense of self-worth. I have seen him masterfully apply the tool of reframing to help people see themselves much differently.

One particular strategy he used was getting these clients to *visualize* the birth of their own child. He would ask them to remember the feelings they had experienced as they held their new born baby for the first time. Of course the response would always be things like, "I was overwhelmed with intense feelings of love."

He would then ask them: "What did the baby do to earn or deserve your love? What great thing had the baby accomplished to make you feel that way towards him or her? Of course, the answer is, the baby did nothing, except maybe mess himself, but what the baby did or didn't do had nothing to do with why the parent felt such intense love for the child.

What my father-in-law helped his clients understand is that *divine worth* and personal accomplishments have nothing to do with each other. *Divine worth* is innate. It is an inheritance not an accomplishment.

It is amazing that we can separate *divine worth* from accomplishments when it involves our own children, but we struggle to be able to separate the two when we think of ourselves.

Although it is okay to acknowledge that we have big challenges and obstacles that make our dreams seem unreachable, when we are connected to divine intelligence, nothing is too hard, nothing is impossible! We have Divine strength available to us as part of our Divineinheritance.

Exercise:

1. Write out a description of how you see yourself (your old self)

2. Write out a description of how God sees you. (Your new image) If you struggle with this think of your new-born baby.

3. Write out your new vision of yourself.

Re-write your life story

"Whatever we plant in our subconscious mind and nourish with repetition and emotion will be realized. Plan it, think about it repetitively. Be emotionally tied to it, and it will become a reality. The subconscious will propel you to figure out a way to accomplish your desires by creating a game plan to achieve them."[58]

It is our job to see it and experience it in our minds and spirits. It is not our job to figure out how to do it, that is the domain of Universal powers. It is our job to feel exhilarated by the whole process; to live in the magic of life.

What are your old stories? Are they stories of lack, emptiness and defeat in any area of your life? If so, the following steps will assist you in re-writing your life story.

Step one: Go to a quiet spot where you will not be disturbed or interrupted. Close your eyes and repeat aloud (so you may hear your own words) the written statement of the thing you want to manifest, the time limit for its manifestation, and a description of the choices you intend to make. As you carry out these instructions see your desire as already manifested.

For example: suppose you intend to write a book that sells 500,000 copies by the first of January, two years from now, that you intend to create the greatest possible value with the content of your book. Your written statement of your purpose should be similar to the following:

"By the first of January . . . , I will have sold 500,000 copies of my book, which will be sold in various increments during the interim. In return for this success, I will create the greatest possible value.

"I believe that this desire will manifest in my life. My faith is so strong that I can now see the sales numbers for the book before my eyes. I can touch it with my hands. It is now awaiting manifestation at the time, and in the proportion that I create the value. I am awaiting a plan by which to accomplish my desire, and I will follow the plan when it is received."

Second: Repeat this program night and morning until you can see your desire manifesting in your imagination.

Remember, as you carry out these instructions, that you are using affirmations for the purpose of giving orders to your subconscious mind. Remember, also, that your subconscious mind will act only upon instructions that are emotionalized, and handed over to it with "feeling." Faith is the strongest and most productive of the emotions.

These instructions, at first, seem abstract. Do not let this disturb you. Follow the instructions no matter how abstract or impractical they may seem. The time will soon come, if you do as you have been instructed, in spirit as well as in act, when a whole new universe of power will unfold to you.

Write Your Script

"You will never rise above the image you have of yourself in your mind."

Your self-image is much like the self-portrait; it is who and what you picture yourself to be. Your mind will complete the picture you tell it to paint of yourself. If the image you have of yourself is limited, when your Divine Purpose calls you to something big, there will be dissonance.

Every person has an image of himself or herself. The question is: does your image of who you are resonate with your Divine Purpose?

Remember the power of agency! It is your responsibility to choose your focus. Choose not to focus on limitations, weaknesses or even your current reality. Visualize the reality of your Divine Purpose! See yourself as who you really are, connected to the Source of unlimited power.

I am statements

I found this post on Facebook. The source of the statistics is unknown. However, I think it give a fairly accurate depiction of what our chances for success will be based on the words we use. Our words are an indication of our mental focus. The words we use in our self-talk and to others are very important. Because words are energy, they can either enhance or hinder our capacity to succeed. Here is a list of commonly used phrases and the probability of success that comes by using them.

- I won't = 0%
- I can't = 10%
- I don't know how = 20%
- I wish I could = 30%
- I want to = 40%
- I think I might = 50%

- I might = 60%
- I think I can -70%
- I can = 80%
- I am = over 90%

Whether these statistics are perfectly accurate or not, it is demonstrates a Universal truth, that our beliefs, thoughts and emotions are energy and there is great power in using statements beginning with the words "I Am."

Here are some examples of how you can use "I Am" statements:

"I am aligned with my Divine Purpose!"

"I am worthy."

"I am abundant."

"I am blessed."

"I am inspired."

"I am living my dreams."

Ask "Why?"

Because our Reticular Activating System has the power to filter through billions of bits of information in order to find what is most relevant to you, a great next step is to ask yourself "Why" in relation to each of your "I am" Statements. For instance, ask yourself, "Why am I aligned with my Divine Purpose?" "Why am I worthy?" "Why am I living my dreams?" This allows the Reticular Activating System to go to work in your behalf, searching for evidence that each of your "I am" statements is true.

I recommend writing down each of your "I am statements" and then re-phrasing them as "why" questions. Then write down each of the reasons or proofs as your RAS reveals them to you. These evidences or proofs will strengthen your belief system, thus affecting the frequency of your thoughts and emotions.

How to write your script

In order to write your life's script, let's start by looking at some of the major areas of your life. For this example let's use: relationships, money, health, career, home and self (Feel free to create others). Write a paragraph about the results you want to create in that area of your life. Then write another paragraph scripting out a visualization of that area of your life as if it is already accomplished.

Here is an example of my own script:

1. Relationships

<u>I will create</u>: A huge network of people who appreciate, and are drawn to, the value I am creating in their lives; a genuine interest in knowing, loving and helping people; abundant opportunities to socialize with so many friends, associates and partners, and close intimate relationships of unconditional love.

<u>My new Script</u>: I have huge networks of friends, followers and people who are drawn to me. People are powerfully attracted to me; they see me as the nicest guy on the planet. I add massive value to their lives. I change their belief systems and empower them to find their life's purpose. I find great joy in making a huge impact on people's lives. I have fun with people.

2. Money

<u>I will create</u>: A life filled with exciting opportunities to add massive value to people's lives; ways to help them fulfill their purposes; multiple and massive streams of income, flowing easily, from things that inspire me.

<u>My new script</u>: Money is pouring in from many abundant streams and opportunities. It is really easy and fun to make massive amounts of money doing things that inspire me; things that are fun; things I love doing. Time seems to not exist when I do them. It doesn't feel like

work at all. New and exciting opportunities are coming to me faster than I can imagine. The value I create for others comes back to me many times over. I have sown seeds in amazing abundance, and I am reaping a harvest that is beyond comprehension.

3. Health

<u>I will create</u>: Alignment, radiant health, peace of mind, inspiration, energy, joy, enthusiasm, fitness and balance.

<u>My new script</u>: I live an inspired life. I live at a peaceful pace. I experience joy and balance. I am energetic, balanced and aligned with my divine purpose. I feed my body with natural foods that produce optimal health and energy. I love exercising.

4. Career

<u>I will create</u>: Excitement, passion, great expectations, and many streams of abundance; abundant networks, abundance mentality, and opportunities flow continuously.

<u>My new script</u>: My career is a blast! I am so gifted at it! I am so thankful for my amazing passionate work! I impact people's lives on a massive scale. I have huge networks of people who are changing their beliefs and finding their purposes because of my gift to them. I love writing books that connect people to God and their divine purpose. Opportunities to speak, motivate, train and inspire people flow to me in abundance. The demand for my speaking and training services is massive. Opportunities to learn new truths that will impact people's lives are all around me. I absolutely love my career. It is booming with success! My work makes a positive difference in the world. People rave about what I do. I feel so fulfilled. This is my purpose for being here! My work is an expression of who I am. It thrills and inspires me and everyone it touches! I am so blessed!

5. Home

<u>I will create</u>: A place each family member loves to be, a place of love and acceptance, a place that friends and loved ones desire to visit, a place that is beautiful, organized and peaceful, a place of joy, a place that reflects who we are, a place that enhances the self-esteem of those who live there.

<u>My new script:</u> I love my peaceful, beautiful home. I absolutely love living here! It makes me feel so nurtured, so at peace, so safe and secure. My home is my haven. I take such pride in my home. When I walk into my home I feel like I'm receiving a warm embrace. It is my peaceful sanctuary. I wouldn't want to live anywhere else. My home is a reflection of me and it's just beautiful!

6. Myself

<u>I will create</u>: A new image;van energy level that impacts all that come in contact with me; a powerful countenance of optimism, faith and expectancy.; radiant joy, abundance and inspiration;   someone who people are changed by; powerful transformational energy and hope.

<u>My new script:</u> I love how I feel. I love that I am constantly focused on this new image. I am handsome, fit and healthy. I have a radiant countenance. I possess amazing confidence. I powerfully inspire people. I am healthy, fit and happy. I beam with the image of victory and success.

Summary

How do I apply this principle?

- Create a clear vision of your end result
- Create your mental movies
- Create your new script

What are the benefits?

- Seeing the realization of your Divine Purpose

- Experiencing the emotions of your Divine Purpose

- What are the consequences of not applying it?

- Go to my website at www.PrinciplesofDivinePurpose.com for a link to mind movies

- Go to my website at www.PrinciplesofDivinePurpose.com for a link to John Assaraf's "innnercise"

CHAPTER SIX

How to Experience "The Flow" of Inspiration! Principle #6: Inspiration

"I never had to choose my subject- my subject rather chose me."

— Hemingway —

While Imagination allows you to see your destination, inspiration reveals the specific steps to be taken. Inspiration is "the flow" of divine intelligence.

Randy Pausch

When Randy Pausch got the news that he was dying of pancreatic cancer, he didn't react the way most people would expect. Randy decided to spend the last few months of his life speaking to people about his life's lessons. He called it the "last lecture series."

Instead of entertaining any kind of self-pity, he spent his remaining months inspiring people to pursue their childhood dreams.

He said: "If you live right, your dreams will come to you. You can't control the cards you are dealt, but you can control how you play them. Decide to be happy! Decide to be grateful!

Rather than sitting around moping about his impending death, he was carrying out his call to inspiration – his Divine Purpose.

His greatest inspiration for writing his "last lecture" was not for the people who came to hear him speak, it was for his three children, so that when they were older they could watch and know the principles their father lived by.

"Throughout various stages of life, inspiration is the thought or idea reconnecting us to the energy we were part of prior to becoming a microscopic particle. I call this "Surrendering to our destiny and allowing ourselves to hear the call." At this point we can differentiate between the demands of our ego and those of ego-dominated people and institutions that deflect us from the call of inspiration. As we move deeply into spirit, we cease to be guided by the ego demands of others or ourselves. We surrender to the always-present force that urges us to be in the blissful state of inspiration. We're guided by our ultimate calling, which is truly our life purpose."[59]

Many people today are stuck in a rut, but it's not because they aren't talented, it's because their vision is limited. They are stuck because they can't see beyond their current circumstances. They don't have an inspired vision of themselves accomplishing their dreams, being promoted or living healthier. They just see more of the same because that's what they're focused on. What inspires you is what you're going to move toward.

The truth is we all have a vision. Every one of us has a picture in our mind of our self, our family and our future. The question is: what does your picture look like? Do you see yourself rising higher, overcoming obstacles, living an abundant life? Do you dare to dream beyond your circumstances?

Today, why don't you change your focus? Lift your eyes beyond your current circumstances. Get a higher dream, a greater vision for your life. See yourself the way God sees you and move forward in the abundant life He has prepared for you!

Why are you trying to Motivate Yourself?

Inspiration is flowing energy that is unseen by the human eye, and the power with which it is felt is undeniable proof of Source Energy, resonance and Divine Purpose. Inspiration is *evidence* that the bandwidth to your Divine Purpose is wide open.

Inspiration connects you to True Success in a manner that can't be experienced in any other way.

Divine Purpose flows as you "let go" of your "outside-in" desire to just take action, and begin taking inspired actions.

Why try to motivate yourself to do something that doesn't inspire you? Instead, why not follow your innate dreams and passions, allowing inspiration to enable the innate gifts and talents that lie within. When this formula is followed motivation is not necessary. When inspiration flows it will compel you to take the actions that are "meant to be." The most truly successful people in the world have always had an inspired dream or vision that compelled them. It is always a joyful and passion filled experience they can't keep themselves from doing. And it was always aligned with their innate gifts and talents. It was never something they had to motivate themselves to do

"Many writers, artists, and musicians have talked about having the experience of suddenly tapping into this dimension of their being where they could see the whole painting already done, or sense the whole book already done, or literally hear the completed song playing – and all they had to do was be a channel for it or take 'divine dictation'. The word 'human' actually comes from a Sanskrit term meaning 'the dispenser of divine gifts'. And that is what we're here to do — to draw these patterns from the invisible and dispense them on earth. Michelangelo knew this when he created the David. He saw the completed masterpiece already in the block of marble and just chipped away everything that wasn't David. He based his life on the idea that these divine perfect forms already existed and his job, rather than creating something out of nothing, was to reveal this heavenly perfection on earth. The universe is not a vast sea of random energy moving in arbitrary ways; there is order, intelligence, and divine ideas waiting to be caught and brought to shore. That's why an acorn always becomes an oak, a caterpillar doesn't become a cat, and we can discover laws that always work. As Einstein said, 'God does not play dice with the universe." – Derek Rydall

There are many ways to get inspiration; some people get a warm feeling inside, some people actually get goose bumps, but the key is that when you are inspired, you feel joy.

Like Thomas Edison said, "when your vocation becomes your vacation, then you know you're where you're supposed to be."

Here is a meditation that I learned from Jack Canfield that you can use to assist you in receiving inspiration. I like to think of it as connecting to Higher-power. This exercise is designed to help you receive a symbol that will teach you about your Divine purpose. I recommend recording the mediation so you can visualize the words as you listen to them.

Begin by creating a meditative place, a place with no noise, lower the lights if it helps, and get into a comfortable position. I recommend having a pen and paper with you so that you can write down your insights after you're done.

Close your eyes and begin taking deep breaths, in through your nose and out through your mouth. Bring shoulders up around neck and squeeze tight, hold it for a few seconds then let go of all the tension in your muscles. Concentrate on rise and fall of you abdomen as you breathe.

Imagine you are sitting in a theatre. At the front of the theater is a stage, and on the back of the stage is a screen. As you look at the screen, the lights begin to dim.

You're going to ask the question, "What is my Divine Purpose?" And the answer will come on the screen in the form of a symbol. Wait patiently until you see an image appear on the screen. Once you see an image appear, ask what the meaning of this symbol is.

You can ask as many questions as you need to. Feel free to ask what the next step is for you to take in your journey.

Notice the symbol on the screen, it may start to move. Ask for a more clear explanation, it will answer.

Now allow yourself to come back to the present moment. Remember, you can come back into this theater at any time and ask questions and you will get the answers.

Now, take your pen and notebook and write down the insights you received.

When you discover your Divine Purpose it will be like a huge weight has been lifted off your shoulders!

A lot of people don't think they have a Divine Purpose because they think it has to be this great, huge thing like eliminating Cancer, or something like that. Your Divine Purpose could be a passion placed in your heart to learn sign language and work with deaf people. It could be a desire to join an organization that builds homes for people in third-world countries. Whatever it is for you, it will be something that resonates with your true self and brings you joy. Often we get talked out of our Divine Purpose when we're children, so we go about life trying to fulfill our ego rather than our soul.

Each of us has an internal guidance system that tells us when were off course (dissonant). Your feeling state of joy is one of those inner guidance systems. Joy is a critical part of your feedback system that tells you if you're on purpose or not. I don't mean feeling it every minute, but a deep feeling of contentment, that you're finally walking the path that was always meant for you.

There is no need to "motivate yourself" when everything you need for True Success and Divine Purpose is already inside you. When you are feeling joy, that is your God-given feedback system that says: "You're on Purpose!" Some of the emotional pain we experieince, is feedback from that same guidance system saying "you're off purpose." It is critically important to follow your inner guidance system and do what feels joyful. The core of your Divine Purpose lies in creating more joy in the lives of other people.

No such thing as laziness, just a lack of inspiration

I know a young man who really didn't like school, and although he was one of the most intelligent young men I knew, he underachieved. Not only did he not like school he also didn't seem motivated to work at menial jobs.

When he got to college he eventually dropped out. His parents and teachers were concerned about his apparent lack of motivation, but the reality was that nothing they were presenting to him aligned with who he was created to be.

From the time he was very young, he had been making movies with the family video recorder. He would get the neighborhood kids together and create a movie almost every day. This was not work to him; this was play.

A few years ago I observed him connect with his purpose and passion as he created his own film business. I saw the lights go on as he aligned with what truly inspired him. I saw him work harder than other young men his age as he built a business around his innate abilities and interests. Because he was inspired, it was not work to him, it was play – it was his purpose and passion!

I observed as he spent almost every spare moment engaged in "self-education." He thirsted for the knowledge that pertained to his new venture. He was inspired and he was taking inspired action in a massive way.

The key here is that he began taking action that he felt inspired to take, not just doing what others told him he "should" do.

"When we're inspired we're connected to this force that's greater in every respect than our physical being. It was in-spirit that our purpose was laid out and it's in-spirit where our magnificence is absolute and irrefutable. Before merging into form, we were a part of God, with all the inherent qualities of a Creator who sends forth abundance, creativity, love, peace, joy and well-being."[60]

Your thoughts and emotions are more powerful than your actions

When you align with Divine Purpose you are led to the right actions. Inspiration is the result of your connection to Divine Purpose. Our thoughts are more powerful than our actions because inspired-thoughts will always lead to the inspired-actions. Actions taken without inspired-thought are often an exercise in futility and result it actions without true power. All great discoveries or creations originated through the power of inspired-thought.

Once you understand the importance of a clear, un-corroded connection to your Source, you are going to begin experiencing the power of inspired thoughts and feelings. When you are inspired, you've established resonance with divine energy. Knowing that thoughts are things made up of vibrational energy, we can now see that inspired thoughts are especially powerful things, because they flow from our Source and put us on a path of divine intention.

Inspiration is Divine Purpose revealing itself to you. Living an inspired life is living in harmony, or, in oneness, with the divine source from which you originated. We could call it "spiritual mindedness." As you seek to live an inspired life you begin to see yourself aligning with your Divine Purpose.

Napoleon Hill understood this concept when he said: "An intangible impulse of thought can be transmuted into its physical counterpart by the application of known principles."[61]

Inspired Action

Anyone who has done work of a creative nature knows the feeling of being inspired. It is an incredible experience when ideas just seem to flow. It's like a faucet has suddenly been turned on. Inspired thoughts and ideas begin streaming into your mind as they did for George Frederick Handle when he composed the Messiah. Sometimes the ideas flow so quickly it is difficult to even write them down, but you know you have to take action.

"Inspired action" is the universe's way of alerting you to an opportunity to create an outcome that is meant for you. When you consistently focus on certain outcomes that are aligned with your purpose, like having more abundance, having your dream career, having a successful business and so on, you start drawing forth all of the resources, people, and opportunities that can help you make those outcomes a physical reality. And many of those resources show up in the form of inspired ideas, or inspired "actions" that you can take.

Many personal development programs are based solely on taking massive action, and of course without action there can be no results. We cannot reap, unless we sow, but if we're frantically sowing the wrong seeds we will not reap the desired harvest. True Success happens when we take actions that are inspired by our Divine Purpose.

When our thoughts and feelings are vibrating in a low, uncomfortable, negative place, we are not open to receive inspired ideas. We are only open to receive problems, challenges, and negativity.

By working consistently on raising our frequency we become aligned with wonderful outcomes! And when we align with wonderful outcomes, we receive inspired ideas that help make those outcomes our reality.

When we are inspired by our Divine Purpose, all of our thoughts break their bonds, our mind transcends limitations, our consciousness expands in every direction and we find ourselves in a new world. Dormant forces come alive and we find ourselves being far greater than we've ever dreamed.

When we're inspired we're in a state of absolute faith – an inner knowing that it's impossible to fail, a complete absence of doubt. We're incapable of thinking limited thoughts. We go beyond the world of boundaries to a place of creative knowing. We are under the guidance of Divine Purpose.

Why Motivation Doesn't Work!

I have always enjoyed listening to motivational speakers. One particular speaker that I really liked, told a story about an audience member who approached him and said "I don't believe in all this motivation stuff." He, of course, replied by asking: "why not?" to which the man said "because motivation just wears off." The motivational speaker quickly retorted: "so does a shower but it's a good idea to take one once in a while." The audience member made a great point. Motivation is a temporary state that needs to be continually renewed. Inspiration is different - inspiration is life-changing.

Motivation is an "outside-in" focus.

Motivation is getting a hold of an idea and taking it to its logical conclusion and not letting anything get in the way of that. We say a motivated person doesn't let obstacles stop them and doesn't allow anyone to interfere with them, because they are highly directed toward a certain goal. Inspiration is the complete opposite. Inspiration is when an idea gets ahold of you and takes you where you were originally intended to go in the first place. It's very different than motivation.

When people have asked me if I am writing another book, I have sometimes said "I don't know, but I think so." And there have been times when I've been trying to write out of motivation and other times when the inspired idea got a hold of me and knew I was called to complete something planted in my soul.

There is something greater in our lives, and when we connect to it, it will take us where we are intended to go.

Wolfgang Amadeus Mozart

Mozart didn't have to motivate himself to write symphonies, because symphonies presented themselves to him "Wolfgang Amadeus Mozart penned **41 numbered symphonies** during his lifetime (and about 25 more were discovered later). He wrote the first one when he was just 8 years old! In fact, before he turned 20 he had written a few dozen"[62]

When an idea gets a hold of you, you get into a place of surrender, where you just "let go and let God." Allow this spirit to compel you into directions you are willing to submit to.

We all come into this life with something to accomplish, and no matter how much others try to motivate us to do what they think we should do, it just doesn't work because we were intended to find that which inspires us. We have to align and connect with our own Divine Purpose and that comes through living an inspired life.

We don't have to write symphonies in order to fulfill our Divine Purpose; we just have to listen to the something deep inside us that is saying "you must do this. This is your purpose." It could be adopting and child. It could be starting a business. It could be starting a charity. It could be any of a myriad of things that we are being called to do.

Why Compulsion doesn't Work!

Compulsion is the reason so many "so-called" successful people spend their entire lives pursuing a dream someone else gave them only to end up in misery, surrounded by trophies they don't care for.

Todd Marinovich was very creative, artistic and shy little boy. He was the son of a former NFL Football player, whose obsessive aspiration was to make Todd into the perfect NFL quarterback. Todd's father completely controlled every detail of his life, including his diet, his training and his performance.

Because of his father compulsion, Todd was never allowed to discover his own purpose and passion. Instead, he was pushed into the limelight of a college and professional football career.

Todd reached the pinnacle of college football success when, as a freshman, he led the USC Trojans to a victory in the Rose Bowl, Unfortunately, even with all the accolades and glory, something was missing – he felt empty inside.

Not only was Todd forced in the direction his father wanted him to go, but he was also made to feel that his passion for art was not valid as a career choice.

In his emptiness, Todd turned to drugs as an escape from the pressure of having to be someone he never wanted to be, and soon found himself trapped in addiction.

Todd's life is a tragic example of how compulsion never leads to True Success. As parents, we need to be careful not to impose our dreams and passions on our children at the expense of their Divine Purpose. We may never fully understand the power of a child's inner desire to have their parents be proud of them, even when it goes against who they were created to be.

Compulsion is the opposite of inspiration. For years I practiced the belief that "successful people do the things that unsuccessful people aren't willing to do." This belief is based on EGO and in my life it was the cause of "dis-ease." It drove me to "frantically maneuver," or make desperate attempts to force things that weren't in alignment with who I am. This is the opposite of a life of flowing inspiration.

People who "franticly maneuver," are people with an "outside-in" focus. They have chosen to take "uninspired action" because of their drive for success that is myth-based. They eventually find that they do not "feel good" or "feel God" because their actions are uninspired.

They are busily working but never really getting anywhere because the things they are engaged in are uninspired, and they find no joy in doing them. They are living without passion and purpose, because their thoughts and feelings are vibrating at a low, uncomfortable, negative place that only attracts more of the same.

In my personal coaching career, I worked with a woman who was convinced that network marketing was her way to success. So we set up goals, milestones and action steps to be taken each week. However, each week when she reported back on her progress, she confessed that she had not completed any of the action steps she committed to the previous week. Upon delving into her beliefs, thoughts and emotions, it became clear that she disliked everything about network marketing. Because she was trying to force herself to do something that didn't inspire her, there was no flow of energy and, of course, no True Success.

Why inspired action does work!

In chapter one, we talked about finding that one thing that really brings you joy; that thing that inspires you, and doing it every day. Doing this daily is almost like a meditative experience, as you enter your state of bliss. Other things just seem to fall away, and you are present, you are in the moment. That's where inspiration comes from.

And when that inspiration comes you act on it, without questioning it, without analyzing it, without trying to figure out where this is going, you just trust that the Universe it giving you something that resonates with that state of passion that you are feeling when you are doing it. Your intuition and inspiration will take you exactly where you want to go it you will just honor it and trust it.

It isn't any harder for the universe to manifest something small than it is for it to manifest something huge. But often the huge things start as a small idea or act of kindness.

Alexandra "Alex" Scott

Before alex was one year old she was diagnosed with Neuroblastoma, a type of childhood cancer. On her first birthday, her parents received the news that even if she beat cancer she would probably never walk again. Just two weeks later, Alex slightly moved her leg at her parents' request to kick. This was the first indication that she was a very determined and inspiring child that had a strong sense of Divine Purpose.

Before she had reached the age of two, Alex could crawl and learned how to stand with the help of leg braces. She worked hard and seemd to be gaining strength as she learned how to walk. It appeared that she was beating the odds, until the bad news came that her tumors were beginning to grow again. On Alex's fourth birthday, she received a stem cell transplant and told her mother, "When I get out of the hospital I want to have a lemonade stand." Her plan was to raise money for doctors to allow them to 'help other kids, like they were helping her. Just as she said she would, she set up her first lemonade stand later that year with the help of her older brother and raised an amazing $2,000 for "her hospital."

Even while she battled her own cancer, Alex and her family

continued to hold yearly lemonade stands in her front yard to benefit childhood cancer research. News of her amazing dedication to other child spread quickly. People from all over the world began to set up their own lemonade stands and donate the proceeds to Alex and her cause.

At the age of eight Alex passed away, knowing that her life had a purpose! With the help of others, she had raised more than $1 million to help find a cure for the disease that took her life. Her Divine Purpose will carry on through her family and supporters around the world are committed to continuing her inspiring legacy through Alex's Lemonade Stand Foundation.[63]

Keep in mind that your current reality is only the result of the vibrational alignment you've experienced up to this point in your life. Your current reality will change as your vibrational connection changes. People look at their current state of affairs and say: "this is who I am." It is not who you are; it is who you were.

Summary

How do I apply this principle?

What are the benefits?

Having the steps of True Success revealed to you

What are the consequences?

Living an uninspired life

Not knowing the actions you came into this life to take

CHAPTER SEVEN

How to Experience Mighty Change
Principle #7: Transformation

"All great changes are preceded by chaos."
~ Deepak Chopra

This quote encapsulates the effect that Divine Purpose has on your life – it transforms you!

True Success is a transformational process. It is a victorious progression toward the fullness of your Divine Purpose. It is a process that strips away everything that keeps your True-self from emerging and aligning with your Divine source. Once you are living these principles you are ready to ask yourself some important questions that will help you see if the Principles of Divine Purpose have transformed your life into True Success.

Many of us know of people who seem to have achieved success in one area of their lives, but seem to have missed out on the most important element of True Success – Divine Character.

Divine character – the Divine Purpose in your refiner's fires

Although the flow of resonance feels effortless and joyful, the process of Divine transformation may not. Part of being transformed is being refined, and refinement requires the intense heat of the refiner's fire.

The story of Corrie ten Boom is a story of a person whose life was deeply transformed by her innate ability to sacrifice the comforts of life to help a people she hardly knew, without regard to their differences in faith and culture. It is a story of someone who had aligned with her highest good - a divine energy that resonated with the goodness of God.

Corrie ten Boom was a Dutch Christian who followed her Divine Purpose. She was true to that which brought her life the deepest meaning, her faith in God and her desire to serve her fellow man. Although her path took her through deep trials, it brought the highest form of True Success, that of Divine character. Corrie and her family, helped many Jews escape the Nazi Holocaust during World War II. Her family was arrested in 1944 because of an informant, and her father died 10 days later in Scheveningen prison. A sister, brother and nephew were released, but Corrie ten Boom and her sister Betsie were sent to Ravensbruck concentration camp, where Betsie died. Corrie has now written many books and has spoken frequently in the post-war years about her experiences. She also aided Holocaust survivors in the Netherlands.

In May 1942, a well-dressed woman came to the ten Boom door with a suitcase in hand. She told the ten Booms that she was a Jew and that her husband had been arrested several months before, and her son had gone into hiding. As Occupation authorities had recently visited her, she was afraid to return home. She had heard that the ten Booms had helped their Jewish neighbors, the Weils, she asked if she could stay with them as well. Corrie's father agreed. He was a devoted reader of the Old Testament, and believed Jews were God's chosen people. He told the woman, "In this household, God's people are always welcome."

This is how the ten Booms began "the hiding place." Corrie and sister Betsie began taking in refugees, some of whom were Jews, others members of the resistance movement who were sought by the Gestapo and its Dutch counterpart. While they had extra rooms in the house, food was scarce for everyone due to wartime shortages. Every non-Jewish Dutch person had received a ration card which was required to obtain weekly coupons to buy food.

In case a raid took place,, the ten Booms built a secret room. They built it in Corrie's bedroom, because it was in the highest part of the house. This would give the people hiding there the most time to avoid detection (as a search would start on the ground floor). A member of the Dutch resistance designed the hidden room behind a false wall. Family and supporters brought bricks and other building supplies into the house by hiding them in briefcases and rolled-up newspapers. A ventilation system allowed for breathing. To enter the secret room, a person had to open a sliding panel in the plastered brick wall under a bottom bookshelf and crawl in on hands and knees. In addition, the family installed an electric buzzer for warning in a raid.

Eventually the Nazis learned of the work the ten Booms were doing and arrested the entire ten Boom family. The family was first sent first to Scheveningen prison where their father died ten days after his arrest. While there, Corrie's sister Nollie, brother Willem, and nephew Peter were all released. Later, Corrie and sister Betsie were sent to the Vught political concentration camp, and finally to the Ravensbrück death camp in Germany. Betsie died there on December 16, 1944. Before she died, she told Corrie, "There is no pit so deep that God's love is not deeper still."[1]

Betsie was Corrie's loving, spiritual, kind-hearted, forgiving sister, who stood by Corrie throughout all of their hardships. Her prayers allowed Corrie to humble herself and say, "Lord pay attention to her prayers." Betsie was a thin, sickly woman with a firm foundation of God. She constantly was thankful for what she had. She thanked God in the concentration camp for fleas!

Corrie was released on December 28, 1944. She later learned that her release had been a clerical error. The women prisoners her age in the camp were killed the week following her release. She said, "God does not have problems. Only plans. The Jews whom the ten Booms had been hiding at the time of their arrests remained undiscovered and all but one, an old woman named Mary, survived.

After the war, Corrie returned to Germany, and traveled the world as a public speaker, appearing in over sixty countries, during which time she wrote many books.

Corrie told the story of her family and their work during World War II in her best-selling book, The Hiding Place, which was made into a film by World Wide Pictures in 1975.

After the war, she traveled to 60 different countries, preaching, and through her, many people became Christians. In 1977, Corrie, then 85 years old, moved to Placentia, California. In 1978, she suffered two strokes, the first rendering her unable to speak, and the second resulting in paralysis. She lived as an invalid for the remaining five years of her life, dying on her 91st birthday (April 15, 1983) following a third stroke.

Corrie ten Boom's character was so transformed by her Divine Purpose that the goodness of God flowed through her no matter what the cost. Choose to see that even your greatest trials have Divine Purpose. Like the work of the Alchemist, your Divine Purpose is refining you as Gold, molding you for the highest form of True Success – Divine Character.

Divine Signatures

The path of Divine Purpose is marked with Divine Signatures. Divine Signatures are miracles and blessings that are evidences of Divine Energy. They are spiritual proofs that your Divine Purpose is supported by Divine Love.

We're not supposed to have little dreams or little plans. Your Divine Purpose is to have big dreams! You are supposed to go out into the deep waters that will make available what is in store for you. But understand, when you're out there in the deep, you can't touch the ground. You can't see the shoreline, and at times, it can get a little turbulent.

Your Divine Purpose is calling you into deep waters, but Divine Energy is with you. There true greatness inside of you. When you are in those deep waters, you are not alone, divine help is always there, causing that greatness to come forth.

If you feel like you are out in the deep today, if you feel like you are overwhelmed, remember, you are in the right place. You will see Divine signatures in the deep, and you will fulfill the Divine Purpose that is in store for you.

Wayne Dyer said: "If I feel called to something higher and then do nothing about it, I'll generally find myself experiencing discontentment and disappointment. But when I act upon that calling by being in vibrational harmony with it, and by being willing to share it with as many people as possible, I feel inspired."[64]

As you become more deeply aware of Divine Signatures, you will gain an inner knowing of your Divine Purpose. Deep inside you there is a "knowing" of what your life is to become. Listen to that voice, the one that wants you to know your Divine Purpose.

The Universal Principle of Transformation is the ultimate evidence you were made for more than "good enough." You were made to increase, to excel, to grow and stretch. It provides you with the inspiration to pick up your dreams with a determination to see them through. It's a new day, and Divine Purpose makes everything new in your life.

All of nature seems to testify of this universal principle of transformation. It is as if the plants, trees and flowers are teaching us that "there comes a time when the risk of remaining tight in the bud becomes more painful that the risk it takes to blossom." - Unknown

What is the risk of staying "tight in the bud?" It is the risk of never experiencing the fullness of your creation. You were meant to experience the fullness of your true greatness that only comes about through a mighty change – divine transformation.

Allow your mess to become your message!

"Let God turn your mess into your message!"
– Unknown

Your Transformation Story

Often it is through our struggles that our biggest life lessons come. And our "mess" is how we came to be where we are right now!

Have you ever thought that the mess in your life was a gift? That your mess is where your message in life is? Life gets messy for us all at times. It's not the experience that makes the difference in our lives; it's what we do with the experience,how we process the lessons and the thoughts we choose to give them.

We get to choose how we view every "mess" in our life. We can't always control our circumstances, but we can control what we think and do with them. We can choose to share a piece of ourselves, and the lessons we have learned as we moved through our "mess." Or we can let the mess in our life knock us down and identify us as a victim.... one of life's bad luck tragedies.

Our life experiences have value. People are waiting for you and your message. Trust that within you is your courage to rise up and get moving along your path.

There are some amazingly hard-learned experiences and lessons inside each of us! When we take the scars of our past and turn them into pearls of wisdom we have indeed honored ourselves, and our experiences. When we share the pearls, we honor our purpose. Our story and our message are what other people are waiting to hear!

Erin Gruwell

Maybe the most transformational and inspirational story I have heard is the story of how a twenty-three-year-old English teacher by the name of Erin Gruwell whose sense of purpose inspired her to drastically transform the lives of her "un-teachable, at-risk" students.

Many of her class members where involved in gangs, and had experienced the horrors of gang violence on a daily basis. One day she intercepted a note being passed in her class with an ugly racial caricature, and angrily declared that this was precisely the sort of thing that led to the Holocaust—only to be met by uncomprehending looks. Surprisingly these inner-city kids knew nothing about the Holocaust.

Because she was so aligned with her life's purpose, she took on two additional jobs in order to come up with the money to purchase the treasured books, "Anne Frank: The Diary of a Young Girl," "Zlata's

Diary" and "A Child's Life in Sarajevo" for each class member. She continued working the extra jobs and used the money to take her kids on life-changing educational field trips.

In an effort to help her students feel understood for the problems they face she got each of them to write in a journal about the troubles of their past, present and future. She said that she wouldn't read them unless the students wanted her too, to her surprise, they all elected to have their journals read.

This was the beginning of an eye-opening, spirit-raising odyssey against intolerance and misunderstanding. The called themselves the Freedom Writers as they learned to see the parallels in these books to their own lives, recording their thoughts and feelings in diaries.

When Ms. Gruwell taught her class about Miep Gies, the courageous Dutch woman who sheltered the Frank family, the kids raised funds through a "Read-a-thon for Tolerance" to make it possible for her to visit them in California, where she declared that Erin Gruwell's students were "the real heroes."

Their efforts have paid off spectacularly, both in terms of recognition—appearances on "Prime Time Live" and "All Things Considered," coverage in People magazine, a meeting with U.S. Secretary of Education Richard Riley—and educationally. All 150 Freedom Writers have graduated from high school and are now attending college.

Ms Grewell's alignment with Divine Purpose turned the mess of these student's lives into their message!

This story is a great example of how whatever we continue to focus on expands in our lives. It doesn't matter if it's hate and intolerance, or amazing acts of heroism. Whatever we focus on with any amount of regularity will continue to expand, strengthening its existence and attracting even more of it into our lives. This is how transformation occurs.

My mess and my message

"*When you have a great pain in your life, you need a greater purpose!*"
– Cynthia Kersey

My purpose and passion were a part of my mess. Out of my mess came the potential to make a difference. I learned that once you share your message you never go back. Once the journey of Purpose, Passion and True Success is opened it transforms you!

My mess was the result of years of living in anxiety, mental tension and stress. I was at least as smart and talented as most people. I probably worked harder than most people. I probably had as much, if not more desire to succeed than most people. I read books and participated in all kinds of personal development programs, but nothing seemed to be working.

I was trying to start a business after being laid off from a salaried position. I was stressed out, worried, buried in limiting beliefs and completely focused on the lack I saw in my life

I was trying desperately to recover from losing everything financially and feeling broke, and broken. I felt ashamed about where I was financially compared to other men my age.

I was working so hard with very little results. I was struggling with anxiety, emptiness, and depression. I was broke emotionally, physically, financially and spiritually. I had developed a mentality of lack and scarcity in all areas of my life, and I saw no purpose in any of it.

Sometimes it's difficult to understand why so many difficulties have happened in my life. Yet I can look back over my life and see that they have been for my own experience and my own good. They have served to strip away ego and pride. They taught me compassion, forgiveness, and charity. Everything that comes my way is essential to my Divine Purpose –especially the struggles.

But through it all I came to the recognition that something was wrong; something was blocked. I had been pleading with God for deliverance. I assumed this was God's will for me; to live in lack and struggle.

There were invisible, yet very real, forces at work causing me to unconsciously resist the flow of success. I had heard people speak about victory through a relationship with God.

Even My own religious beliefs were barriers to my ability to align with my Divine Purpose. I experienced nagging emotions of worry, fear, unworthiness and shame that were not in alignment with joy, peace, love. These emotions actually brought illness, anxiety attacks and eventually a heart attack at age 49.

I wasn't a vibrational match to all the goodness that flows from my source (God) – abundance, joy, peace of mind, beauty, kindness.

I decided to see if what was manifesting, or not manifesting, in my life could actually be the result of an unseen scientific or spiritual law so I decided to document my experiences so that I would have a record that could be shared with others.

I came across a science video explaining how everything is made of energy. In other words, everything vibrates. Even the things that we can't see with the human eye vibrate, but do so at different frequencies.

I watched as the scientist in the video put one million volts of electricity through his body without it hurting him, simply by changing the vibrational frequency so that it wasn't in resonance with the human body.

Seeing this, awakened me to the reality that there are "invisible" Universal laws at work that are absolutely real. It opened my mind to the possibility that if beliefs, thought and emotions were really energy I needed to understand how to use these laws in my favor.

As my knowledge grew "line upon line," my understanding expanded and an amazing transformation began to take place as I learned principles like resonance, mind renewal, imagination and inspiration. My vibrational signal began to change from one of anxiety, worry and hopelessness to one of excitement, joy and gratitude. I was becoming a very different person – more purposeful, passionate and truly successful. This transformation brought about this book the "7 Principles of Divine Purpose."

A new frequency creates a new identity

"It's a new day, and Divine Purpose makes everything new in your life."

When you choose to change your beliefs, thoughts and emotions, you undergo a transformation. Some refer to this as being "born again." It is a change of spiritual frequencies that puts you in harmony with God. Jesus taught Nicodemus that he could not see the kingdom of God unless he experienced this type of transformation, one that would put him in resonance with God's presence. The first eight verses of John chapter three read as follows:

"There was a man of the Pharisees, named Nicodemus, a ruler of the Jews:

The same came to Jesus by night, and said unto him, Rabbi, we know that thou art a teacher come from God: for no man can do these miracles that thou doest, except God be with him.

Jesus answered and said unto him, Verily, verily, I say unto thee, Except a man be born again, he cannot see the kingdom of God.

Nicodemus saith unto him, How can a man be born when he is old? can he enter the second time into his mother's womb, and be born?

Jesus answered, Verily, verily, I say unto thee, Except a man be born of water and of the Spirit, he cannot enter into the kingdom of God.

That which is born of the flesh is flesh; and that which is born of the Spirit is spirit.

Marvel not that I said unto thee, Ye must be born again.

The wind bloweth where it listeth, and thou hearest the sound thereof, but canst not tell whence it cometh, and whither it goeth: so is every one that is born of the Spirit." (John 3:1-8)

There are two worlds or realms, the physical realm and spiritual realm. The spiritual realm operates at higher frequencies and cannot be known by the physical senses - they are dissonant. Before we can see or enter this spiritual realm a change must take place that is so fundamental and far reaching that it can best be described as "new birth."

All matter is composed of atoms. The air we breathe though invisible to us is made up of atoms. It is the arrangement of the properties that make things different (solids, liquids or gasses). Any solid is mostly empty space. There is almost unlimited empty space within matter.

Atoms are not solid, instead they are like tiny solar systems composed of infinitely small particles, revolving at tremendous speeds and bound by tremendous forces. Like our solar system, atoms are almost entirely empty space.

If I tried to run through the wall all I would get is a lump on the head. That which would prevent my body from passing through the wall is not a collision of particles, but a collision of forces. Why did God withdraw himself from fallen, sinful man and put a barrier between himself and man? Why did God become flesh and cross that barrier and stand among us? Why did He become flesh and blood like each of us? He did it to provide the way that we might cross that barrier and return to Him. He did it to help us become a vibrational match for His presence, if that is our choice.

Remember, as the vibrational frequency of an object changes, its form also changes. This means that we as human beings can be transformed, by changing our vibrational frequencies – our beliefs, thoughts and emotions. As we take on a new identity, one that vibrates in alignment with our creator and our Divine Purpose.

A New Identity

God has many names that describe His character and attributes. In the same way that someone named "Joe" might also be called "father" or "husband" or "the boss," God has names that describe Him and His relationship to His people.

In the Old Testament, the Hebrew name for "God" was considered so holy that the people wouldn't even say it. So, when God appeared to Moses in a burning bush and sent Him to lead the Israelites out of captivity, Moses asked God, "Who should I say sent me?" After all, He couldn't breathe the name of God in public. God replied by saying, "Moses, my name is I Am." In other words, "I am anything and everything you need. I am your joy. I am your peace. I am your strength. I am your victory. I am your way of escape. I am whatever you need."

Today, God is saying the same thing to us! What is it that you need? The Great I Am, the Almighty God is ready to supply all your needs according to His riches in glory. Open your heart of faith to Him today and receive all the blessings He has in store for you! – Joel Osteen

When you use the words "I am" the Universe goes to work organizing everything for its fulfillment! Who do you say that you are? Be careful how you use the words "I Am." It is so easy for us to buy into the belief system that "who I am is what I do for a living. Who I am is my possessions." Who I am is separate from what I want to **manifest** into my life.

Transformation means no longer using the words "I am" in ways like this:

- I am not lucky
- I am not educated
- I am not smart
- I am not attractive
- I am not talented

This is an "outside-in" focus. It's focusing on what's missing, what's not possible, it's limiting, and it's separating you from your source. Believe it or not it is ego.

Look upon these as absolute facts. You can say them with the same confidence as you can say "the sun is always shinning." Even though there are cloudy days and the sun isn't visible, the sun is indeed always shinning. Use the words "I am" to describe your new identity; who you are "in alignment" with God – your Divine Source.

- I am aligned with my Divine Purpose!
- I am amazingly successful in business!
- I am kind and thoughtful!
- I am radiating high energy!
- I am radiating optimism!
- I am operating at brain wave levels of ease, flow, joy and alignment!
- I am connected to God and the universe with a powerful connection!
- I am a resonating with True Success!

Have you received a new vibration?

Isn't it the Divine Purpose of our creator to transform us, to deliver us and to give us victory? Then wouldn't our Divine Purpose be aligned with His? Isn't our Divine Purpose to experience victory in our own lives so that we can assist others in the same process?

Our creator and source, cannot make us one with Him, or transform us without our permission, without our decision to "come to Him and be transformed by Him?"

His transformation takes place from the "inside-out." It starts by changing our beliefs, thoughts and emotions - increasing the bandwidth by which we are connected to Divine power.

As that bandwidth increases and more Divine power flows and we are changed. The change is so deep and so fundamental that we begin to have a new frequency, a new energy, a new vibrational signal. In essence, we now sing a "new song."

The Evolution of Divine Purpose

I want to encourage you to be open to the constant evolution of your Divine Purpose. Even if you think you already know exactly what your Divine Purpose is, and you have an idea of exactly what it will look like and feel like, you might be pleasantly surprised to see that idea expanding and evolving as time goes on. God might throw a fun curve ball in there, just to improve your own ideas. Don't worry though, as long as you are focused on purpose and passion, the curve balls will be exciting and inspiring. You'll see them as unexpected miracles.

FINAL WORDS

I

It is my hope that these Principles of Divine Purpose will be as transformational in your life as they have been in mine. I also hope that I can continue to assist you in your transformation process.

The True Success Coaching Program

True Success Academy:

To apply these principles at the highest possible levels, you may want to consider the help of the True Success Coaching Academy online training course. . To learn more about True Success Academy go to www.PrinciplesofDivinePurpose.com.

RESOURCES AND REFERENCES

1. Wayne Dyer, Inspiration, (Carlsbad, CA, Hay House, 2006), 28

2. Deepak Chopra, The Seven Spiritual laws of Success, (San Rafael, CA Amber-Allen Publishing, 1994), 95-96

3. Richard Paul Anderson, Your Divine Purpose, (American Fork, Ut. Covenant Communications, 2008),

4. Deepak Chopra, The Seven Spiritual Laws of Success, (San Rafael, CA Amber-Allen Publishing, 1994), 2

5. Deepak Chopra, The Seven Spiritual Laws of Success, (San Rafael, CA Amber-Allen Publishing, 1994),   54

6. Deepak Chopra, The Seven Spiritual laws of Success, (San Rafael, CA Amber-Allen Publishing, 1994), 76

7. Timothy Ferris, The Four-hour Work Week, (New York, Crown Publisher, 2007), 4

8. Carrie Wilkerson, Barefoot Exectutive, xvi

9. Deepak Chopra, The Seven Spiritual Laws of Success, (San Rafael, CA Amber-Allen Publishing, 1994), 85-86

10. Deepak Chopra, The Seven Spiritual laws of Success, (San Rafael, CA. Amber-Allen Publishing, 1994), 88

11. Garrett B. Gunderson with Stephen Palmer, Killing Sacred Cows, (Austin, Tx. Greenleaf Book Group, 2008), 3

12. Jack Canfield, The Success Principles, ( ), 19

13. The inspiration Show, http://www.mindmovies.com/ inspirationshow/index.php?episode=198

14. Napoleon Hill, Think and Grown Rich, ( ) 155

15. Joel Osteen, Your Best Life Now, (New York, NY. Faith Words, 2004), 72-73

16. Katrin Prentice, A Key Ingredient to reaching your goals, http://www.coachingreallyworks.com/a-key-ingredient-for-reaching-your-goals/?awt_l=O5mE.&awt_m=3j_72Hd7VTEilh)

17. Napolean Hill, Think and Grown Rich, ( ), 1

18. Earl Nightengale, The Strangest Secret, (Naperville, Il, Simple Truths/ Nightengale Conant, 2005), 38-41

19. Practice—Creating Neural Pathways to Mastery: Part 1, http://salaamhearts.com/advice/59/PracticeCreating_Neural_Pathways_to_Mastery_Part_1

20. Timothy Ferris, The 4-Hour Work Week, (New York, Crown Publisher, 2007), 56

21. Jeffrey Scwartz and Rebecca Gladding , You Are Not Your Brain, (New York, NY. Penguin Group, 2011), 36

22. Jeffrey Scwartz and Rebecca Gladding , You Are Not Your Brain, (New York, NY. Penguin Group, 2011), 37

23. Pablo Coelho's Blog, http://paulocoelhoblog.com/2012/02/13/coelhooffice-07-the-meaning-of-life

24. Earl Nightengale, The Strangest Secret, (Naperville, Il, Simple Truths/ Nightengale Conant, 2005), 35

25. Guest Post Blog, September 11: A Higher Purpose, http://www.guideposts.org/inspirational-stories/september-11-higher-purpose

26. Victor E Frankl, Man's Search for Meaning, (Boston, Mass. Beacon Press, 1959), 66

27. Life Without Limbs, http://www.lifewithoutlimbs.org.

28. Timothy Ferris, The 4-Hour Work Week, (New York, Crown Publisher, 2007), 50

29. Nightengale, The Strangest Secret, (Naperville, Il, Simple Truths/ Nightengale Conant, 2005), 31

30. Nightengale, The Strangest Secret, 32

31. Joel Osteen, Your Best life Now, (New York, NY. Faith Words, 2004), 72

32. Joel Osteen, Your Best Life Now, (York, NY. Faith Words, 2004), 48

33. Joel Osteen, Your Best Life Now, (York, NY. Faith Words, 2004), 101

34. Deepak Chopra, The Seven Spiritual Laws of Success, (New York, NY. Faith Words, 2004), 28

35. Allow Abundance Course Week 18, p.5

36. Spencer Condie, The Song of Redeeming Love, (Salt Lake City, Ut, Deseret Book, 2002), 45

37. Stefan Zweig, The Tide of Fortune, 104, as quoted in Spence J Condie, The Song of Redeeming Love (Salt Lake City: Deseret Book, 2002), 43

38. Spencer J Condie, The Song of Redeeming Love, (Salt Lake City: Deseret Book, 2002), 44

39. Spencer J Condie, The Song of Redeeming Love, (Salt Lake City: Deseret Book, 2002), 44

40. Spencer J Condie, The Song of Redeeming Love, (Salt Lake City: Deseret Book, 2002), 45

41. Joel Osteen, Your Best Life Now, (York, NY. Faith Words, 2004), 129

42. Joel Osteen, Your Best Life now, (York, NY. Faith Words, 2004), 29-30

43. Jack Canfield & Pamela Bruner, Tapping into Ultimate Succcess, (Carlsbad, CA, Hay House, 2012), 3-4

44. Transcenddental meditation Blog, http://www.tm.org/blog/ enlightenment/albert-einstein/

45. Transcenddental meditation Blog, http://www.tm.org/blog/enlightenment/albert-einstein/#sthash.QYfwmxBA.dpuf

46. Quoted in Peter Barker and Cecil G. Shugart, eds., After Einstein: Proceedings of the Einstein Centennial Celebration at Memphis State University (Memphis State University Press, 1981), 179. - See more at: http://www.tm.org/blog/enlightenment/albert-einstein/#sthash.QYfwmxBA.dpuf

47. Transcenddental meditation Blog, http://www.tm.org/blog/enlightenment/albert-einstein/#sthash.QYfwmxBA.dpuf

48. Arthur Zajonc, The Meditative Life, "Practical instruction on how to tap into your mind and heart, plus inspiration from great meditation teachers."

49. Jack Canfield & Pamela Bruner, Tapping into Ultimate Succcess, (Carlsbad, CA, Hay House, 2012), 136

50. Canfield & Pamela Bruner, Tapping into Ultimate Succcess, (Carlsbad, CA, Hay House, 2012), 6-7

51. jyotsna, A Collection of Short Stories, http://jyotsna-collectionofshortstories.blogspot.com/2010/11/heart-of-gratitude.html)

52. Brett Olsen, Zero to Hero, (Tempe, Az. B & B Books, 2012), 23

53. Napoleon Hill, think and Grow Rich, ch5

54. http://www.mindmovies.com/mm21/john_assaraf_visualization.php?16363&ol=11&ac=lp560

55. Joel Osteen, Your Best Life now, (York, NY. Faith Words, 2004), 11)

56. Brett Olsen, Zero to Hero, (Tempe, Az. B & B Books, 2012), 18

57. Joel Osteen, Your Best Life now, (York, NY. Faith Words, 2004), 62

58. Brett Olsen, Zero to Hero, (Tempe, Az. B & B Books, 2012), 23

59. Wayne Dyer, Inspiration, (Carlsbad, CA, Hay House, 2006), 6

60. Wayne Dyer, Inspiration, (Carlsbad, CA, Hay House, 2006), 7

61. Napoleon Hill, Think and Grown Rich, 11

62. http://www.favorite-classical-composers.com/mozart-symphonies.html

63. Alex's Lemonade Stand, http://www.alexslemonade.org/about/meet-alex

64. Wayne Dyer, Inspiration, (Carlsbad, CA, Hay House, 2006), 10

CPSIA information can be obtained at www.ICGtesting.com
Printed in the USA
BVOW02s0535190214

345377BV00010B/344/P